God's Abundant Life

How to experience and nurture it

God's Abundant Life

A simplified version of The Life of God in the Soul of Man by Henry Scougal and Rules *and* Instructions for a Holy Life by Robert Leighton, Archbishop of Glasgow

**Prepared by
Steve Hanchett**

GRACE PUBLICATIONS TRUST
175 Tower Bridge Road
London SE1 2AH
England
e-mail: AGBCSE@AOL.com

Joint Managing Editors:
T.I. Curnow
D.P. Kingdon M.A., B.D.

Consulting Editor:
J. Philip Arthur M.A.

ISBN 0 946462 682

© Grace Publications Trust 2003

Distributed by:

Evangelical Press
Faverdale North Industrial Estate
Darlington
DL3 0PH

Cover design and artwork by Lawrence Littleton Evans
Printed in Great Britain by Cox & Wyman Ltd, Reading, Berks

Contents

Introduction

'Men may write big volumes, and, as one says, talk much and say nothing; but it is a great matter to talk little and yet say much.' Those words were spoken by George Gairden at the funeral of his friend Henry Scougal. Scougal had died from tuberculosis a few days earlier on June 13, 1678. He was only twenty-eight years old.

By all accounts Scougal was a brilliant and devout young man. Early in his life his father, Patrick, had dedicated Henry to the Lord's ministry and his childhood was marked by rapid development both spiritually and intellectually. He memorised large portions of Scripture and learned Hebrew, Greek and Latin as well as other languages. He was skilled in mathematics and history and taught himself the intricacies of philosophy. Scougal entered King's College in Aberdeen, Scotland at age fifteen and finished his studies four years later.

During his brief life Scougal served as a professor at King's College for four years, pastored the church at Auchterless for one year and then returned to King's College where he trained young men for the ministry as the Professor of Divinity. Scougal used every one of these positions to carry out his life's mission of helping others to experience the abundant life that comes through a relationship with Christ.

In his teaching, his preaching, his writing and his personal relationships Scougal was always focused like a laser beam on this one goal – helping others to know Christ and find their happiness in him. Every casual conversation was viewed as an opportunity to plant gospel seeds in people's hearts. Every sermon was prepared, not only by studying the meaning of a Scripture text, but also by studying what words, phrases and illustrations would best communicate the truth to those who would hear the message. Every time he purchased a book he was thinking about someone that might be blessed by its content.

It was Scougal's desire to lead others to Christ that gave birth to *The Life of God in the Soul of Man*. He originally wrote this book as a letter to a friend with the hope of seeing him come to a true faith. Some of Scougal's friends read the letter and were so moved by its contents that they gave a copy to bishop Gilbert Burnet with the request that he consider having it published. Once he had read Scougal's letter Burnet did not hesitate to grant the request. One cannot imagine that Burnet could have known the far reaching impact of the decision to publish Scougal's letter.

The list of people whose lives have been influenced by this book reads like a 'Who's Who' in church history. John Newton, the author of the hymn 'Amazing Grace,' counted this as one of his favourite works. More recently, J.I. Packer wrote the foreword for an edition of *The Life of God* and John Piper's *The Pleasures of God* was inspired by Scougal's work.

Susanna Wesley, the mother of John and Charles Wesley, was so moved by this book that she encouraged her sons to study it. John did and this study helped to shape his belief that Christianity is first and foremost a religion of the heart and soul. John was so taken by Scougal's presentation of the gospel that he joined his mother in asking Charles to read Scougal's writing. It must have made a deep impression on Charles also because when his friend, George Whitfield, was struggling to find peace with God this is the book that Charles gave him to read.

God used *The Life of God* to open George Whitfield's eyes to see that all his religious works could never save him and that he needed the new life that comes through Christ.

Whitfield, speaking about this incident in his life, said, 'Though I fasted, watched, and prayed, and received the sacrament so long, yet I never knew what true religion was till God sent me that excellent treatise by the hand of my never-to-be-forgotten friend.' Years later in a sermon Whitfield recounted that experience by saying, 'I must bear testimony to my old friend Mr Charles Wesley. He put a book into my hands called "The Life of God in the Soul of Man," whereby God showed me that I must be born again or be damned.' Whitfield, of course, became that mighty instrument of God in the Great Awakening that brought multitudes into the kingdom of God. The message that he preached was the message that he first learned by reading *The Life of God in the Soul of Man*.

This writer first became acquainted with the name Henry Scougal through the writing of John Piper and the biography of George Whitfield. I first read *The Life of God* wanting to find out what it contained that so powerfully influenced the lives of so many people. Frankly, the archaic language and sentence structure proved to be a barrier to fully understanding the author's intent. To overcome that barrier I borrowed a very old English dictionary and set out to translate Scougal's words into modern English. Over the course of a couple of years I worked my way through *The Life of God* numerous times. Every rereading brought new insights and blessings. Scougal's writing is a beautifully fresh look at what it means to experience the abundant life of God.

At this time in history many people have religion, but few seem to have real spiritual life. Scougal speaks directly to this problem and clears a path for others to walk in the fullness of God's life. It is my sincere hope that a modern translation of his work will have the same life transforming effect as did the original writing.

Though Scougal's life was a brief twenty-eight years, the influence of his life is immeasurable. To again quote from George Gairden's funeral message, 'length of life is not to be measured by many revolutions of the heavens, but by the progress we have made in the great design for which we are sent into the world … he has lived much in a few years and died an old man in eight and twenty years.'

Attached to Scougal's writing is a brief work by Robert Leighton (1611-1684) entitled *Rules and Instructions for a Holy Life*. It seems fitting to put these two works together. Leighton greatly influenced Henry Scougal. Leighton lived through a turbulent time in church history. Throughout his life there was an ongoing struggle between the Presbyterian and Episcopal leaders in Scotland for supremacy in the church. His father had been a Presbyterian minister who was persecuted for his views and who persecuted others for theirs.

Robert first began his ministry as an ordained Presbyterian minister but after becoming disenchanted with some of the actions among his peers be received Episcopal ordination. Leighton's ultimate goal was to find the best in both systems and unite them in one church. It was a frustrating experience for Leighton, one which he finally abandoned.

The legacy of Robert Leighton's life is not that he changed the world in which he lived, but that the world in which he lived did not change him. He lived his life in the eye of a storm and yet he remained a man of deep spirituality and moral integrity. He never sought personal power and he conducted himself at all times honourably toward others. He never attempted using force or coercion to change other people. He considered persecuting others for their views to be 'scaling heaven with ladders fetched from hell'.

Leighton believed deeply that what people needed was true inward spiritual life. It was Leighton's passion for heartfelt religion that, in part, influenced the thinking of Henry Scougal. What was important to Leighton can be heard in his response to a question asked once about the content of his preaching. When he was asked why he wasn't preaching about the issues of the day he replied by asking who was preaching those things. He was told that all the brethren were doing so. To that he answered, 'If you all preach up the times, you may surely allow one poor brother to preach up Christ Jesus and eternity.'

That truly was the desire of Robert Leighton's life – to make Jesus Christ known and to find life in him. The vision and heart of Leighton finds a kindred spirit in Henry Scougal. Therefore, it is fitting that these two men should find their works together in this volume calling people to experience, not just religion, but abundant life in Jesus Christ.

Steve Hanchett 2003

PART 1

How to experience abundant life

Henry Scougal

1.
True Christianity

My Dear Friend,

Our friendship gives you the right to expect my greatest effort to serve your needs. Don't think it is a burden for me to try to meet them. Your deepest needs are spiritual, and as it is my life's calling to help others grow spiritually, ministering to you brings me great joy.

I am sure that there is better help available than what I can give. I will probably not say anything you didn't already know. Still, I hope that you will accept this letter since we are friends. My prayer is that God may so direct my thoughts that the words I write will be helpful to you.

I want to start by sharing some thoughts about what a Christian is. I am confident you already know these truths, but I want to start here in order to give you a good foundation to build upon.

1. Mistaken ideas about Christianity

It makes me sad to think that many people who claim to be Christians don't really know what that means. Some people think that they are Christians because they have accepted the beliefs of a particular church. But the only testimony they have is that they belong to a particular church or denomination.

Other people think they are Christians because of their good works. They think that since they live at peace with their neighbours, don't eat or drink too much, go to church, say their prayers, and help the poor occasionally, they have satisfied God.

Still others think that they must be Christians because they have had deep emotional religious experiences. They always try to pray fervently and they hope to have their thoughts of heaven result in deep feelings. They think that Christ will receive them because of their emotions. They are persuaded that their emotions prove that they are deeply in love with him. To them the only proof they need of their salvation is their feeling that they are saved.

Knowing the truth, doing good works, and having emotional experiences are indeed a part of the Christian life, but they should not be mistaken for salvation itself. At best these things are fruits of the Christian life, but they are not its root.

There are many imitations of true Christianity. Even sinful attitudes and actions can be passed off as true Christianity. I don't mean the false worship of the heathen. That is obviously not Christian. What I am referring to are people who consider themselves Christians even though they don't live as Christians should.

They pretend their sins and evil desires are really good things. They act as if their cutting words and pride are evidence of their Christian seriousness. They pretend that their fierce wrath and their bitter anger are really holy zeal. Further, they make believe that when they are rebelling against those in leadership and authority they are displaying Christian courage and resolve.

2. What Christianity is

True Christianity is altogether different from what I have been describing. Those who actually know Christ will reject all imitations of true faith. *True Christianity is the union of the soul of man with the life of God.* It is an actual sharing in the life of God. Christianity is having the very image of God painted on the soul. In the apostle Paul's words, it is 'Christ in you' (Colossians 1:27). The best two words I know of to describe the nature of true Christianity are *divine life*. These two words are the basis for what I am writing to you about true Christianity. First, I want to show you why I describe it as *life*. Second, I will show why it is called *divine*.

True Christianity is eternal life

I have chosen to describe Christianity by the word *life* first of all because it endures. Even if a person has emotional experiences and does good works, if it doesn't last it can't be called true Christianity. Most people think that they must do some good works in order to save their souls. People who become convinced of this often change their lives very quickly. But these same people soon get tired and give up.

They start out with passion but their zeal soon cools off. They do good works and they seem to be growing. But like a plant without roots they quickly wither.

These sudden religious fits are like the actions of a beheaded chicken. It runs around doing things, but it can't keep it up because there is no life in it. In contrast, the actions of a true Christian are faithful and enduring because they originate in the everlasting life of God.

This life of God in the soul of man does not always have the same degree of strength and power. Christians experience times of spiritual decline and they struggle with temptations. They are not always cheerfully ready to obey God. But even in times of spiritual decline the life of God is never extinguished and Christians are never enslaved by the love of the world.

True Christianity is life in the heart

Christianity can also be described by the word *life* because it is an inward power inhabiting the heart. The Christian's works are produced by the life of God in the soul. The Christian does not do things because he is forced to by something outside of himself. Christians are not driven to live for Christ by threats of punishment, nor by being bribed by promises. Instead, they have an inward desire to do good and find joy in doing it.

The truly spiritual person doesn't love God and goodness because it is commanded. He loves God because he has new life in his soul. This new life teaches him and moves him to

18

love. The Christian doesn't pray because he is forced to. He doesn't read the Bible to avoid God's wrath. He doesn't worship God to quieten his accusing conscience. He does these things because having received this new life, he finds pleasure in his fellowship with God.

The spiritual person does not pray and repent simply because they are commanded. He does so because he wants to. He has experienced God's grace and he knows the problems and misery that come from a sinful life. He is not forced to be generous. His giving is not extorted from him. His love to God produces a willingness to give. Even if there were no duty to give his heart would devise 'generous things' (Isaiah 32:8).

Lack of self-control, injustice or any other vices are contrary to the nature of the new life in Jesus Christ. These sins are as out of character to the Christian as would be unkindness to the most kind heart or immodesty to the most modest person. The apostle John was right when he said, 'Whoever has been born of God does not sin, for His seed remains in him; and he cannot sin, because he is born of God' (1 John 3:9).

Godly Christian people do not ignore the law of God. They hold it in high regard. But it is not so much the threat of punishment that moves them. They obey because they see how pure and good and reasonable the law is. They consider the law excellent and desirable in itself. They know that in keeping it there is great reward. God's love makes them become a law unto themselves.

> Who shall prescribe a law to those that love?
> Love is a more powerful law which moves them.

What Jesus said of himself is in some ways true of his followers: 'It is their meat and drink to do their Father's will' (see John 4:34). It is only natural to have an appetite for food. We desire to eat even if we are not thinking about how food sustains our physical life. In the same way, the true Christian has a natural, unforced desire for that which is good and right.

It is true that things outside of ourselves can help make us want to live spiritual lives. This is particularly true when a person is still spiritually immature and weak. A spiritually immature person may not be able to grow without being pushed forward by his fears or problems. It may be that he needs authority, the law, or the influence of other people to move him toward maturity. If an immature Christian is faithful and steady in his obedience he will grow into maturity. If he sincerely hates his spiritual weakness and truly wants to serve God with zeal and passion, God will honour his first faltering steps of spiritual life even if they are weak.

On the other hand, a person who isn't experiencing this kind of life and doesn't desire it cannot be called a Christian. A person who acts 'spiritual' only because of his training, tradition, a fear of hell or unspiritual notions of heaven, can no more be called a Christian than a puppet can be called a man. Forced, artificial Christianity is apathetic – without vitality. For people who are coerced into the Christian life, living it out is like lifting heavy weights over their heads.

20

Their faith is cold and without spirit. They act like a woman who has married someone she doesn't love, but carries out her role because of a sense of duty.

This nominal Christianity is stingy and selfish. When it comes to doing things contrary to their natural desires, nominal Christians will resist. People without God's life do only what is absolutely required of them. Since they are motivated by the law, they do only what it demands and no more. In addition, they will interpret the law in ways that give them the greatest possible liberty to do what they want.

The true Christian gives of himself freely. True Christianity has nothing like the narrow, legalistic, calculating spirit that does just enough to get by. But the person who has committed himself entirely to Christ will never think he does too much for him.

True Christianity is divine life

By this time I hope it is clear that it makes sense to define Christianity as *life*. I hope that it is also clear why it is vitally important to differentiate between it and the spirituality that is coerced and that depends upon external causes. At this point I want to explain why I describe it as *divine life*. The reason I call it this is not just because God is the source of this life. Without a doubt God is the author of this life. Men are born again by the power of the Holy Spirit. But it is also called *divine life* because of its nature.

The true Christian mirrors God's nature. Christianity is the glory of God shining in the soul of man. It is an actual sharing of his nature. It is a beam from the sun of God's eternal light. It is a drop from the ocean of his infinite goodness in the soul of man. Those who are truly Christians have 'God dwelling in their souls' (see 1 John 4:12), and 'Christ formed within them' (see Galatians 4:19).

3. What the natural life is

Before I write about the divine life in more detail it might be helpful to briefly describe the natural life. My understanding of the natural life is that it is characterized by our desire for things that are pleasing and acceptable to our nature. The root of the natural life is self-love. This self-love sprouts up and produces as many fruits as there are desires and bents in men. The natural man is controlled by the physical senses. He lives his life by sight and not by faith. He makes his decisions based upon whether he thinks some action will bring him pleasure or pain.

These natural desires are not all bad in themselves. They are really examples of the Creator's wisdom. God gave his creatures desires that help preserve their lives. In animals these desires serve as a law that helps them carry out the purpose for which they were created. But we should remember that man was made for a higher purpose than animals. Therefore, he is to be guided by higher laws. So when a man is governed by his natural life only, and he neglects the higher purpose for which he was created, he becomes guilty before God.

It is not that our natural desires are to be completely ignored or crushed. But they are to be controlled and ruled by the spiritual life. In other words, the difference between a Christian and a non-Christian is that the Christian is controlled by the divine life and the non-Christian is controlled by the natural life.

The character of the natural life

It is interesting to see in how many different ways the natural life expresses itself. People often make the dangerous mistake of thinking they are spiritual when they compare themselves to others. What they fail to see is that their good works and the sins of the people they compare themselves to come from the same root. This becomes obvious if one considers that much of what is passed off as true Christianity is really the outcome of people's natural disposition.

Some people are naturally light-hearted and cheerful. As a result, they often do things that seem silly to others. Other people are serious and conservative. The way they act makes some people assume that they are very spiritual and righteous. Still other people can be mean, harsh and bitter. They can't be happy and they will not allow anyone else to be either. Some people have a sweet spirit and are kind. They enjoy the company of friends. To these people it is really important that others like them. It is a good thing God made people like this. They make up for a lack of true charity in the world since they are more inclined to do things to help others.

Training and education should also be considered. Some people's behaviour has nothing to do with their relationship to Christ. They act the way they do because that is how they were raised. Again, some people were never taught to follow any rules. They do whatever brings them pleasure and gives them some personal advantage. On the other hand, some people were taught to be decent, honourable, and virtuous. Because of their training they are almost incapable of doing anything that they were taught is wrong or immoral.

There are vast differences in men's make-up. Character is a result of natural strengths or weaknesses, and intelligence or wisdom; and whether or not a person uses or neglects these gifts.

We know that lust, injustice, cruelty and ungodliness are the result of self-love. These wicked things are the fruit of the natural life when it is not conquered by Christ nor controlled by natural reason. But if a natural man has common sense, good judgment, and intelligence he may very well reject these sins. He might even seem to be virtuous and holy. If he has enough sense to realize the damage sin and lust will do to his health, possessions and reputation his self-love may be enough to restrain his sinful desires. He may even recognize that treating others fairly is the best way to protect his own interests and reputation.

It should also be noted that this natural life might even cause a person to be so moral that his goodness will look very much like godliness and true Christianity. A non-Christian may even want to study theology. That can be as pleasing and satisfying to the natural life as any other kind of study. The natural life may also produce a zeal to maintain and promote religious teachings as well as to convert others. Since effective public speaking is enjoyable no matter what the subject is, the natural man may enjoy hearing and writing sermons about Christianity.

In some people the natural life may even motivate them to develop a devotional life. Other people fall in love with the idea of heaven when they hear about its beauty. The descriptions of heaven in the Bible can easily affect a person's desires. These descriptions can make a person want to be there even if he doesn't understand the spiritual pleasures these pictures represent. A person may even feel affection for Christ when he hears that he has purchased the benefits of heaven for him. He might even convince himself that he really loves Christ even though he is still a stranger to him.

The point is that people often appear to have spiritual life when in truth they don't. Their good works and other people's evil works may be coming from the very same root of self-love. The good works and the evil works of men without Christ flow from the very same fountain.

It is important to consider this natural life. Even the Christian needs to understand that many achievements in life are a result of talents he was born with. The natural life along with intelligence and reason helps him experience prosperity. I don't wish to condemn these things in themselves. I just think it is important to consider their nature so as to keep things in perspective. This helps us not to value ourselves because of our successes or to place our hopes for heaven in our human works.

4. How the character of divine life is manifested

At this point I want to go back to look at the nature of the divine life. This is the 'life that is hidden with Christ in God' (see Colossians 3:3). This life isn't showy and the world doesn't pay it much attention. To the natural man this life has little value and is a boring subject. He thinks like this because he is self-centred and his life is geared toward his own sinful pleasures. In contrast the spiritual person is not captive to a self-centred love. The divine life holds sway over his natural desires and keeps him from being enslaved by things that he knows are wrong.

The divine life is like a tree whose root is faith. This tree produces the fruits of love for God, charity toward man, and personal purity and humility. As one wise man said, 'Even though these things are common and everyone talks about them so much that everyone is bored with it, they still are so important that neither men nor angels could speak about anything more important.'

The root of the divine life is *faith*, and its chief fruits are love to God, love to man, purity and humility. Faith is to spiritual life what the senses are to the physical life. Faith helps one perceive spiritual realities. Through faith one can comprehend all spiritual truth. Because of our fallen state our faith especially holds fast to God's promises of mercy and redemption for sinners through Christ the only mediator between God and man. True faith is resting in Christ. Therefore it is called 'faith in Jesus Christ'. The first fruit of the divine life is *love for God*. This love produces a joy and delight in God's glory. It creates within a heart that is willing to surrender and sacrifice itself completely to God. The highest aim of the person who truly loves God is to please him. The person with this love is willing to suffer anything if it brings God glory. Nothing is more pleasant to one who loves God than to have fellowship with him.

When a person first becomes a Christian he may love God only for what he receives from him. But in time his love for God will grow and mature and have higher motives. The young Christian will eventually come to love God simply because God is good and great and worthy of being loved.

The second fruit is *love for our fellow humans*. A person who has been captivated by the love of God will also come to love all men and women unconditionally. This is only right since all people are created in God's image. It is through this fruit of the divine life that people learn how to treat others. The man who truly loves others will be deeply concerned about their welfare. When other people are injured or wronged this person will be so concerned that he will take offence as if it had been done to himself.

Purity is the third fruit of the divine life. It could be defined as a person having a heart that hates sin and rejects it, even if it would bring him some pleasure. A person with a pure heart will sometimes even deny himself things that are not necessarily sinful. If he thinks something will quench his desire for righteousness or decrease his joy in pursuing the things of God, he will avoid it. It can also be implied that the person who longs to be pure in heart will patiently endure any hardship necessary to remain faithful to God. If this is true, then purity means not just having self-control and being moral, but being courageous and sacrificial as well.

The fourth fruit of the divine life is *humility*. Humility opens our eyes to see ourselves as we really are – unworthy sinners. A truly humble person sincerely bows before God to confess that all he is and all he has is a generous gift from him. Humility always produces deep submission to God's will. True humility delivers us from loving this world's praise and men's applause.

Faith, love, purity and humility are the highest attributes that men or angels could possess. The person who has these spiritual fruits has the very foundation of God's nature laid in his soul. This person does not have to pry into God's secret decrees or search the books of heaven to know his eternal destiny. Instead, he finds God's thoughts about him written on his own heart.

The love of God in his heart will give him assurance of his relationship with God. The joy he experiences as he submits to God's will and is transformed into Christlike character is a sure sign of true life. It testifies that his joy will be perfected and will continue throughout eternity. With good reason someone once said, 'I would rather see real evidence of God's nature on my soul than have a vision from heaven or an angel sent to tell me that my name is written in the Book of Life.'

28

5. Christ's life portrays the life of God

We can never say enough fully to teach the mysteries of the new nature and the divine life. Mere words alone are not enough to describe these things. New life in Christ can only be fully understood by those whose hearts have been made alive to enjoy spiritual things and given light to see the truth of God in Christ. 'There is a spirit in man: and the inspiration of the Almighty giveth them understanding' (Job 32:8, AV).

The life and power of Christianity are seen more clearly in actions than in words. Actions are more powerful than words and more accurately evidence the inward life that produces them. Because of this, these spiritual fruits are best understood by observing the actions of truly spiritual people. And the best way to know if these fruits are in us is to compare ourselves with the perfect example of our blessed Saviour.

One of Jesus' aims during his incarnation was to teach, by his life, what he expected from others. His life perfectly portrayed what he demanded of others. If ever true goodness was visible to human eyes it was through the example of his life.

Christ's love for God

Christ's heart constantly burned with a sincere, deep love for his heavenly Father. He expressed his love for his Father by submitting to his Father's will. Doing the will of God and finishing his work was like life-giving food for Christ

29

Jesus not only obeyed his Father in adulthood, but even in childhood he was absorbed with doing the Father's will. During his life on earth Jesus never considered his travels or trials to be too great a cost for doing his Father's will. To the contrary, doing God's will brought contentment and satisfaction to Jesus' heart.

For example, once Jesus was weary from a long journey and rested by a well. While there he asked a Samaritan woman to give him a drink of water. Their conversation quickly turned to a discussion about the Kingdom of God. This discussion about spiritual things brought such joy and strength and refreshment to Jesus' spirit that he forgot how thirsty he was. He was so refreshed that he didn't even want to eat the food his disciples brought him from the city (John 4:4–34).

Not only did Jesus delight in the will of God, he lovingly submitted to it with patience even when it required him to suffer. Jesus endured the most severe troubles and extreme misery ever inflicted on a man. Even so, he never complained or became discontented.

Jesus went to the cross knowing full well how much he would suffer there. But he didn't approach the cross like a fanatic or a fatalist. He felt pain as much as any other man. The sweat and sorrow of Christ in Gethsemane make it clear that he knew how great his suffering would be. In spite of all this he still completely submitted to the sufferings of the cross.

It is true that Jesus prayed 'if it is possible let this cup pass from Me' (Matthew 26:39). But he also prayed, 'not my will but Your will be done'. In this connection our Lord's words recorded in John 12:27-28 are significant. This passage is the first place we find Jesus acknowledging his spiritual distress. He said, 'Now is my soul troubled' (AV). This would seem to indicate he wanted to delay or avoid the cross. He also prayed, 'Father, save Me from this hour'. This was a prayer for deliverance. But no sooner had Jesus made this request than he withdrew it by praying, 'But for this purpose I came into the world'. And Christ's true intent was revealed when he prayed, 'Father, glorify Your name'. He was committed to seek God's glory even if it meant he had to suffer.

Don't think that these prayers are evidence of wavering or weakness in Jesus. He knew all along what he was going to suffer agony yet he boldly accepted his destiny. What these prayers do make known is the incredible burden and pressure that Jesus had to bear. His suffering was so awful and against his nature that he couldn't think about it without horror. Still, he not only accepted his suffering; he desired to suffer so that God could receive glory.

Another evidence of Christ's deep love for his Father was the delight he found in prayer. Jesus often would go away by himself and enjoy spending the whole night in prayer. He prayed like this even though he had no sins to confess and very few physical needs to pray about. Unfortunately these are almost the only things that drive us to prayer.

We could say that Jesus' whole life was like a prayer because he was in constant communion with God. Even when he was not offering the sacrifice of prayer, he always kept the fire burning on the altar. Jesus was never overcome by the spiritual deadness or lukewarm spirit we so often struggle with before we can pray.

Christ's love for humanity

I would like to tell you everything possible about Christ's sacrificial love for people. But I can't since that would require me to write the whole history of his life and comment on it. Every act and word of Jesus seemed to be done for the good and benefit of someone else. His miracles displayed not only his power, but his kindness as well. Not only did they amaze those who saw them, they helped the people upon whom they were performed.

Jesus' love was not reserved just for his fellow Jews, his family or his personal friends. On the contrary, everyone who obeyed his word was loved as if they were family. This is why he said, 'whoever does the will of My Father … is My brother and sister and mother' (Matthew 12:50).

Anyone who came to Jesus with sincere motives was always welcomed by him. He never denied any request that was for the good of those who asked. No one ever went away from Jesus sad except the young rich ruler. But he was sad because he couldn't save his soul and his money too. Even in this Jesus displayed his love. It troubled him that even though eternal life was offered to the young man he did not have the heart to receive it. The young man's question about eternal life revealed an openness that attracted Jesus' love. For it is recorded that 'Jesus beholding him loved him' (Mark 10:21, AV). Yet even though he loved him, Jesus would not make a new way to heaven. After all, should Jesus overthrow God's created order that makes it impossible for a greedy man to be happy?

How can I possibly describe the love Jesus displayed when Judas betrayed him with a kiss? And what further evidence is necessary to prove his fervent, infinite love than that he laid down his life for his worst enemies? While his blood was being poured out he prayed for these foes. He pleaded with the Father not to hold his death against them. Instead, he prayed that his death would open the way to eternal life for the very people who crucified him.

Christ's purity

As I said before, the third fruit of divine life is purity. Purity requires rejecting this world's pleasures. To be pure compels us to persevere since there will be temptations to be faced. If anyone was ever totally free from slavery to the pleasures of this world it was Jesus. He occasionally enjoyed these pleasures when they came his way but he never went out of his way to seek them.

For example, Jesus gave others the freedom to enjoy married life. He showed his approval of marriage by attending a marriage ceremony. But for himself he chose to live a single life. As another example, at the same wedding Jesus miraculously provided for the lack of wine. But he would not do a miracle to relieve his own hunger in the

33

wilderness. Jesus was gracious enough to allow others freedom to enjoy lawful pleasures and godly enough to abstain from them himself. He was willing to provide for the less significant needs of others as well as their more serious needs. The Bible tells us many times about Jesus' suffering and pain but it never says he laughed and only once that he rejoiced in spirit. His life exactly fulfilled Isaiah's prophecy that he was 'a Man of sorrows and acquainted with grief' (Isaiah 53:3).

The trials and discomfort Christ experienced were all matters of his choice. No person ever had more ability to exalt himself to the highest position in the world. A person who can miraculously gather fish into a net and take money from a fish's mouth to pay his taxes could easily make himself the richest man in the world. Jesus power was so great that he could have assembled an army large enough to overthrow Caesar even without money. His miracles clearly demonstrated the extent of his great power.

But Jesus made it clear that the things of this world were relatively unimportant to him. His life was so humble he could say, 'foxes have holes and birds of the air have nests, but the Son of Man has nowhere to lay His head' (Matthew 8:20).

Jesus did not spend his time with the rich and powerful. Instead he was known as the son of a carpenter who had fishermen and poor people for his friends.

Christ's humility

Now, I want to direct your attention to Christ's humility, the final fruit of the divine life that I want to discuss. Jesus was the greatest example of humility who ever lived. Through him we learn to be 'gentle and lowly in heart' (Matthew 11:29). It is not my intention to write about the humility that was involved in the eternal Son of God becoming man (but see Philippians 2:5-11). I only want to consider his humble behaviour while he was in this world.

It is only right for sinners like us to be humble. But sin was not the reason for Christ's humility. He was so captivated by the Father's infinite glory that in his human nature he was nothing but God's servant. Jesus taught that the glory of God which shone forth from his life was a gift from God and not his own (see John 17:22). He did not claim this glory originated in himself and humbly renounced all claims to it.

Jesus refused to be greeted by the rich young ruler as 'good master'. It seems the young man was ignorant of Christ's deity. Jesus asked him, 'Why do you call Me good? No one is good but One, that is, God' (Luke 18:19). We see from this question that the young man thought of Jesus as only a man. So, accommodating his reply to the young man's ignorance of his deity, Jesus makes it clear that man does not deserve to be praised for God alone is good.

Jesus never used his miraculous power for show or public display. He would not satisfy the curiosity of the Jews with a sign from heaven. Neither would he listen to those who wanted him to do miracles in a way that would draw attention to himself. Even when his love prompted him to heal someone, in humility he sometimes asked the one healed not to tell others what he had done. At times it was necessary for him to do miracles publicly. He did so when it fulfilled God's will and brought God glory. But he always gave the entire honour to his Father by telling everyone that 'the Son can do nothing of Himself' (John 5:19).

It is impossible here to retell every example of Jesus' humility. We would need to speak of his withdrawal when people wanted to make him a king (John 6:15), his child-hood obedience to Mary and Joseph (Luke 2:51), and his submission to all the suffering he endured from his enemies (see Matthew 27:26-31). The history of his holy life is full of examples like these. The best way to learn humility and the other fruits of the divine life is to diligently study his life.

At this point I want to suggest a prayer. I hope this prayer will be helpful to those who have had mistaken ideas about Christianity but have now begun to see the truth.

6. A prayer for Christlikeness

Father, you are infinite and majestic. You are the Creator of all life and the source of all joy. Still, we sinners know so little about you and how to please you. We talk about Christianity and pretend we are Christians, but so few of us really know what that means. We easily mistake the desires of our old nature, and the works we do out of self-

love, for spiritual life. The truth is only your grace can make us acceptable in your sight. My sorrow is justified. I have wandered for so long in a land of empty shadows of holiness and false images of faith.

I praise you that in your love you have begun to open my eyes and let me see what I ought to be. I rejoice that you have the power to change my heart. And I am glad that you produce righteousness in those you chose to save. How wonderful is your mercy in sending Christ to teach us by the example of his life what we ought to be! Oh, may the holy life of Jesus always be in my thoughts until I become like him. Let me never cease to seek him until the divine life prevails in my soul and Christ is formed within me. Amen.

2.
The excellence of abundant life

Now, after learning the true nature of Christianity, the best thing we can do is reflect on its excellence and benefits. When someone discovers how great the Christian life is he or she can't help but diligently pursue it. Words cannot describe how great the joy of the Christian life is. This joy can only be understood by those who experience it: 'a stranger does not share its joy' (Proverbs 14:10).

Holiness is the life and health of the soul that has been saved by God. The person without Christ is spiritually weak and not able to function as God intended. He is weary and restless. But when Christ gives new life to him he receives both a new strength in his soul and peace in his heart. His mind can now understand what is good, and his will can cling to it. No longer is his heart chained to his physical senses and the influence of others. Instead he is controlled by God's Spirit and moved by faith in things unseen.

1. The excellence of loving God

Let us consider one of the specific aspects of the fruit of the divine life – the love that binds Christians to God. We want to see how superior love is and the joy it brings. What we love is what we consider to be most important in life. As a result, whether or not we have true joy depends on what we love.

Further, the worth and value of our soul is measured by what we love. If we love corrupt and wicked things we become corrupt and wicked. But the person who loves God spiritually grows and matures until he becomes like the One he loves. What a person loves is constantly on his mind. And what we think about has a power to transform our soul. We become like what we behold.

We see this principle in action when we see lovers and friends unknowingly imitating the people they love. Without knowing it they begin to look like each other. They become similar in actions, speech, gestures, and dress. It is natural to copy the characteristics of the people we love. This is a good thing when we imitate their virtue and holiness. But since all men have good and bad qualities we are constantly in danger of imitating the bad character of others. When we love the wrong things we will become contaminated and corrupted by them. Love can easily blind us and cause us to approve of, and then imitate, the things that are wrong in others.

The best way to improve ourselves is by fixing our love on God's perfections. We should keep him always before our eyes. By doing this we will become like him. 'We all, with unveiled face, beholding as in a mirror the glory of the Lord, are being transformed into the same image from glory to glory' (2 Corinthians 3:18).

The person who sincerely and passionately keeps his eyes on the beauty and holiness of God will become a very different person. His soul will become different from the rest of the world. Worldly things will lose their appeal. He will not cherish corrupt and immoral thoughts that diminish his desires for God and his righteousness.

Love is the greatest thing we have. Therefore, it is foolish and wrong to give love to that which is not worthy. Love is the only thing that we have that we can call our own permanent possession. Other things can be taken from us by force, but no one can steal our love. In giving our love we give our all. In giving love we give over our hearts and wills, by which we possess all other pleasures. Love by its nature is giving. The value of a gift is measured by the heart of the giver. The person who loves gives all that he is to the person he loves. This love brings happiness to the person loved.

Because of the nature of love, God is the One whom we should love supremely. Certainly, love is the greatest gift we can give to God. It becomes very corrupted when we give it to another. But even our misplaced love expresses itself in ways that point to the fact that it was meant for God.

For instance, the flattery we direct toward others is the language meant to be directed toward God. People often use words when speaking to celebrities that should be used for God. Without question, a person who treats someone else as a god would be wiser to give his love to the One who really is God. Humble words of complete submission are debasing when spoken to men. But these same words are exalting when spoken to God. The chains of love which bind a heart to God are far better than liberty. Being enslaved to God in love is more noble than being a king in this world.

2. The advantages of loving God

Loving God exalts a person's soul and it is the only thing that can make a person truly happy. The greatest pleasure and delight a person can experience comes from the joy of loving God.

On the other hand, love ends up becoming bitter and full of pain when we give it to someone who is not able to receive it and is not grateful enough to respond to it. Love also brings us heartache when those we love are absent from us. Further, we hurt when those whom we love experience hurt. So when we love people like ourselves we open ourselves to all kinds of painful experiences. But our love for God does not have these problems.

God is worthy of our love

I believe that when we love people who are not capable of receiving or returning it we will experience misery, trouble and worry. Love is such a powerful passion that it will torment a man's spirit when it does not find it returned. Love, by its very nature, is so boundless that we have to limit and restrict its capacity when we give it only to other people. Only in loving God do we give our love room to stretch itself to its full potential and apply its full strength and power. So how can a little skin-deep beauty or some small degree of goodness satisfy a passion that was made to be given to God and designed to embrace him?

When a man and woman fall in love they do not allow any rivals. They know their hearts do not have room for two lovers. That is why the Scriptures say that 'Love is as strong as death' and it results in 'jealousy as cruel as the grave' (Song of Solomon 8:6).

But love for God does not face these difficulties. Once our love is fixed upon God it is satisfied by his abundant glory and goodness. Really, our love is too small for such a great God. Lovers of God are sorry that they are not able to love him more. They wish they had the fiery love of angels and long for the day when they will be able to love God with a pure, complete passion. Since they are unable to love enough by themselves they desire the aid of the whole creation. Those who love God want every angel and man to join in praising and loving him.

God returns our love

When love is not appropriately returned we know sorrow and not joy. Love is the most valuable thing we can give away. In a sense we give all that we have to the one we love. Because of this it is extremely painful to have this great gift rejected. It hurts when the gift of our whole heart has not won another person's heart and been returned.

Perfect love is a kind of self-abandonment and self-sacrifice. Love requires us to die to ourselves and our own interests

42

for the sake of the one we love. To love a person we must sacrifice ourselves to please him. Because of this high price love demands we become quite upset if love is not returned or the person we love does not pay us any attention.

But if the person who gives his love has that love returned he experiences new life. He finds his own life in the life and interests of the person he loves. He begins to think of his own interests, not because they are his, but because the person he loves cares about him. He becomes dear to himself because he is dear to the person he loves.

But why should I expound further on this well-known truth? Nothing could be clearer than the fact that the happiness of love depends on having it returned. Therefore, the one who loves God has a huge advantage. He has given his love to One whose nature is love, whose goodness is infinite, and whose mercy preserved us even while we were his enemies. How much more will God embrace us when we are his friends! It is impossible to think that God would deny his love to a person who is totally devoted to him and desires to serve and please him. God cannot despise his own image or the heart on which he has imprinted it. Love is all that we can pay him. Love is the sacrifice that God will not despise (see Psalm 51:17).

God will never leave us

Separation from the people we love makes us unhappy and causes turmoil. When friends part company, even for a short time, they experience affliction of heart. It is sad to be deprived of the company we enjoy. When the one we love

43

leaves us our life becomes tedious. We spend our time impatiently waiting for the happy moment when we will meet again. But what if death is the cause of separation? Sooner or later it will be. This kind of separation brings a grief that is rarely matched by any other misfortune in life. This is the high price we pay for the joy of friendship.

But God is never separated from the people who love him. They only have to open their eyes and they will see the traces of his presence and glory everywhere. They will always be able to speak with the one they love. This truth makes the darkest prison or the most barren desert not only endurable, but delightful.

God gives us true happiness

We know that we are unhappy when the person we love is unhappy. Those who love each other are bound to care about each other's happiness and problems. Because of this, love can bring us trouble when we give it in this earthly life. The most fortunate person has enough problems to disrupt the peace of his friends. It is hard to be at peace when we suffer not only with our own troubles but with the troubles of our friends as well.

But if we loved God above everything else we would experience happiness that would not decrease. We should rejoice to behold the glory of God. We would find pleasure in the praises men and angels give to God. We would be delighted beyond words that the One who loves us is eternally happy and that all his enemies can never shake his joy. 'Our God is in heaven; He does whatever He pleases' (Psalm 115:3).

The person who loves God and submits to his will has a solid foundation for true happiness. True joy comes to the one who only wants to please God. Oh the peace, rest and satisfaction that comes to the one who loves God with his whole heart.

Loving God gives sweetness to all of life

We naturally experience great pleasure when we lose ourselves in God. There is no greater joy than, being swallowed up in such a sense of his goodness, we gladly offer up ourselves as living sacrifices that are constantly rising to God in flames of love. We never know real joy and true pleasure until we become weary of our selfishness and renounce all ownership of our lives and give ourselves unto God. It is in abandonment to God that we become holy. It is then we can truly say from the heart, 'My beloved is mine and I am his. I am content to be anything for his sake. I care only about how I might serve him.'

A person who has a heart like this will find pleasure in all the events of life. Even life's pleasures will have a different flavour when we taste God's goodness in them and see them as tokens of his love. The person who gives himself completely to God finds that even discipline loses its sting. To him the rod as well as the staff can bring him comfort. Therefore, he is ready to kiss the hand that disciplines him and gathers sweetness even from severe chastisement. He rejoices that his plans are not allowed by God. Instead, he finds joy in God's will and wisdom.

Loving God makes Christian service a delight

Many people find living the Christian life to be tedious and unsatisfying. But those who love God discover pleasure and delight in their duties. They rejoice when they are asked to 'go to the house of the Lord' that they may see his 'power and ... glory' (Psalm 63:2). Their happiest moments are when they have withdrawn from the world, with all of its noise and busyness, and have entered into the presence of God to enjoy fellowship with him.

Those whose hearts have been captivated by the love of God discover God to be their greatest joy. They enjoy thinking about him, remembering his mercies, and declaring their love for him. The lay their burdens before him and give him their troubles. Even repentance is delightful when it comes from a heart of love. There is a secret sweetness that accompanies tears of remorse, when they flow from a broken heart that is returning to God.

To live a life of sacrifice, purity, and holiness is trouble-some to those who are ruled only by an external law. But when God's love possesses the heart this guards it against everything that offends Christ, and it refuses to give in to the temptations that assault it. A person controlled by God's love not only obeys explicit commands, but cheerfully follows the gentlest hints of his pleasure. He will even become creative in trying to discover what will be most liked by Christ and most acceptable unto him. To this

46

person self-denial is no longer harsh and dreadful. Instead, it becomes delightful and sweet. This part of my letter is much longer than I originally intended. But who wouldn't be tempted to dwell on such a wonderful subject. I will try to make up for this by being shorter on other points.

3. The excellence of loving others

The next fruit of the divine life that is produced by the life of God in the soul of man is love for others. The greatness of this fruit is obvious. What could possibly be more excellent than a heart that loves the whole world? What could be more wonderful than a person who wants the best for others?

He who loves his neighbour as himself never thinks of harming others. To the contrary, he is always willing to give them what they need. He would rather be hurt himself than hurt someone else. He finds joy when he makes someone else happy. The hatred or ingratitude of others does not keep him from loving them. Instead, he overlooks the pain they cause him and overcomes their evil with good. The only plans he has for his enemies is to help them see their need of Christ.

Is it any wonder that this kind of person is admired and considered the sweetest of men? Even his facial expressions reflect his kind and gentle spirit. Other people are inspired to do good because of his example. Most heroic actions we know of were inspired by a love of country or love of a friend. But a more spiritual and universal love would surely inspire even greater deeds of love.

The pleasure of loving others

When love comes from the heart it produces great satisfaction and pleasure. It is delightful for a man to see his love mature. It brings pleasure to our soul when we see ourselves delivered from malice, hatred and envy. If I had my choice of anything that might produce happiness in me, I would choose to have my heart filled with love for all men. I am confident that this would allow me to partake in all the happiness of others. Everything that benefited them and gave them joy would give me joy and pleasure as well.

It is true that I would still suffer and grieve with others. But there is sweetness in suffering with others that makes it much more desirable than cold insensitivity. And we can lessen our worry about our trouble by meditating on God's boundless goodness and wisdom by which he rules the world. We should also consider that the sorrows of this life might lead others to find the way to eternal life. In that we can find great comfort in sorrow.

Next to the love and enjoyment of God, the passionate love and affection for others is rightly considered the greatest joy of heaven. If universal love prevailed in this world it would be a preview of heaven and we would have a taste of the joys of heaven on earth.

4. The excellence of purity

The third fruit that the life of God produces is what I call purity. You may recall that I defined purity first of all as disdain for the passing pleasures of sin. Secondly, I said it was a commitment to do what is right even if it causes us personal pain.

The worst kind of slavery is slavery to our own lusts. Likewise, the greatest victory is in overcoming those same lusts. A person cannot do anything noble or worthy if he is wallowing in sin or spending all of his time pursuing the passing pleasures of this world. The spiritual man has a God-centred passion. He knows he was made for better things. Therefore, he refuses to step one foot off the path of holiness in order to pursue sinful pleasures.

Purity produces lasting pleasure

The partner of purity is pleasure. Whatever defiles the soul disturbs the soul. All sinful pleasures have a sting in them and leave a residue of hurt and problems. Sin and lust are clearly enemies of the health of the body and the best interests of our lives. A little common sense ought to make any rational man avoid them for that reason alone.

If a person chooses to abstain from harmful pleasures and even rejects lawful ones this should not be looked upon as a harsh choice or an extreme sacrifice. Instead, it should be seen as a better choice that results in the pursuit of God and righteousness. Any person who is engaged in the passionate pursuit of God quickly forgets the pleasures of this world.

Hearts captivated by God's love are not consumed by the pleasures of this life. Even eating and sleeping become secondary. Christians consider those things to be unnecessary for real happiness and the higher pleasures they are pursuing. Even troubles become opportunities to grow and prove their love for God. They rejoice in the honour of suffering for his name.

5. The excellence of humility

The last fruit that the life of God produces is humility. Even though some men consider this virtue worthless, we are not capable of a higher, more noble characteristic. Whilst foolish ignorance gives birth to pride, the truth produces humility. Humility prevents us from loving things that have no spiritual value. It keeps us from admiring ourselves because of some small achievement. The wise man does not value himself because of his riches, good looks or strength. Nor does he despise those who lack these things. The knowledge he has of God's glory makes him realize how small his achievements are. So he keeps striving to conquer himself and become more like Christ.

I do not know how most people define humility, but I do see almost everyone pretending to be humble. They avoid words and actions that make them look proud and arrogant. Even the people who desire praise the most are usually not willing to promote themselves. Are not all of our compliments and kind words our declaration of the value of others and the humble thoughts we have of ourselves? So does it not prove that humility is a noble virtue when even the imitation of it is so common among men?

Humility produces joy

Humility is accompanied by much happiness and peace. But the proud man is trouble for everyone who knows him. Anything can irritate the proud person and hardly anything can please him. He is ready to complain about everything that happens as if he were so important that Almighty God should see to it that he is always happy. He acts as if all the creatures of heaven and earth should wait upon him and obey his will. The leaves of high trees shake with every blast of wind. Likewise, every casual conversation or harsh word will upset and torment a proud man.

The humble person, however, has an advantage. When he is despised no one can think less of him than he thinks of himself. Therefore, he is not troubled by the criticism that would have wounded others. Instead, he tolerates it. Since he is less affected by criticism he is less exposed to it as well. Pride leads a man into a thousand troubles which those with meek and lowly hearts rarely encounter. True, genuine humility gains the respect and love of wise, discerning people. On the other hand, pride defeats its own purpose by depriving a man of the honour he so desperately seeks.

Since humility is first discovered in the presence of God, it is always followed by great pleasure and satisfaction. It is impossible to express the wonderful pleasure and delight that a Christian feels when he humbly bows before God. He has a deep sense of God's majesty and glory. He sinks, if I

51

may say it this way, to the bottom of his being and disappears in the presence of God. Because of his deep understanding of his own nothingness, weakness and sin he understands the full meaning of the Psalmist's words, 'What is man that You are mindful of him?' (Psalm 8:4). The proud person who desires to be noticed does not get as much pleasure from the praise and applause of men as the humble Christian does. For when he is praised he renounces it and says, 'Not unto us, O Lord, but to Your name give glory' (Psalm 115:1).

I have written about the excellence and advantages of Christianity by describing its fruits. But if I pretended to have given a perfect account of it I would be mistaken. We must experience it ourselves and experience will teach us more than all that has been written or spoken about it. Now, if we believe our soul desires this great joy it would be good to express that in this prayer.

6. A prayer for a changed heart

God, what a mighty joy you have called us to! How gracious you are to have married our duty and happiness together and promised us a great reward for doing our duty. Shall foolish worms like us be exalted to such a great height? Will you allow us to raise our eyes to you? Will you accept the affection of people like us? Can we really become like you by beholding and admiring you? Shall we partake of your infinite happiness and glory by loving you and rejoicing in your glory?

Oh, how happy are those who have broken the chains of self-love and whose hearts are free from the love of this world. Happy are those who have their minds enlightened by your Holy Spirit and their wills enlarged to match yours so that they love you above all things and mankind for your sake.

Oh, God, I am fully persuaded that I can never be happy until my sinful desires are put to death and my pride is subdued. Until I seriously despise the world and think nothing of myself I cannot know what real joy is. But when will this happen? When will you come to me and satisfy my soul with your likeness by making me holy as you are holy?

Have you enticed me with the prospect of this great joy without intending to bring it to pass? Have you stirred these desires in my soul without working to satisfy them? I know that you intend to complete this work in me. Teach me to do your will, for you are God. Your Spirit is good. Lead me into the land of uprightness. Quicken me, O Lord, for your name's sake and perfect me. Your mercy, O Lord, endures forever. Forsake not the works of your own hands. Amen.

3.
Difficulties and duties of the Christian life

So far I have written about what true Christianity is and how desirable it is. But I recognize that when someone sees how far his heart is from being what it ought to be, he might just throw up his hands in despair and give up. He might even believe that it is not possible for him to become a Christian. His only response might be to become broken in anguish and bitterness of heart.

1. Overcoming discouragement

This person might say,

> Truly those who have God's life in their souls are happy. But my nature is completely different and I am not able to make such a great change. If my outward actions could have made me a Christian I would have hope since I am diligent and careful. But since nothing but a new heart can produce the necessary change, what can I do?

> One moment I think I could give everything I own as offerings to God or as gifts to the poor, but then I realize I can't make myself love. Therefore, that kind of

sacrifice would mean nothing. If a man would give all his possessions for love the offer would be totally rejected.

I consider making myself miserable and giving myself over to trouble and hardship. But I know that will not starve my evil desire nor will it keep me from loving this world. Sinful lusts are always lurking in my heart. The vain things I have closed the door on are always coming back in through the windows.

I don't question the fact that I am spiritually bankrupt. I know how sinful and dark my heart is. You would think that would make me humble. But instead I am angry and discontented. Even if I were able to think humbly of myself, I couldn't tolerate it if others thought badly of me. As a result, when I think about my greatest deeds I realize that they are only expressions of my carnal nature and the fruits of my self-love. I just disguised them as something better.

My sinful nature is so powerful and its roots run so deep in my soul that I don't think I can ever be delivered from its rule over me. I swing from side to side like a door on hinges but I can never be unhinged from self. Self is still the root of all my actions.

I think the only benefit I get from reading about true Christianity is to stand and look at it from afar. In the distance I see the joy I am not able to have. I am like a man who is shipwrecked in the sea. He sees the shore and the people there. He envies their happiness and comfort but is full of despair because he knows he can't get to the shore himself.

Unreasonable fears

I think that many people who have just begun to understand the true nature of the Christian life feel like this. They have spied out the land and know that it flows with milk and honey. But they also see the giants of lust and sin that stand in their way and they fear they can never overcome them.

Why should we give in to such discouraging thoughts? Why should we allow these fears to dampen our spirits? We should not be throwing these obstacles down on the path that we are trying to walk. Instead, we ought to be encouraging ourselves. We should remind ourselves of the mighty help we will receive in this spiritual warfare. 'For greater is he that is in you than he that is in the world' (1 John 4:4, AV). 'The eternal God is your refuge, and underneath are the everlasting arms' (Deuteronomy 33:27). 'Be strong in the Lord and in the power of His might' (Ephesians 6:10). Surely God himself will 'tread down our enemies' (Psalm 60:12), but we must centre our minds upon the help God has given us.

First, remember that God has a tender concern for the souls of men. He is gladly willing to pursue their welfare. He has humbled himself for our sake. He has sworn an oath that he has no pleasure in our destruction. No such thing as malice or envy lodges in the heart of God. His nature and name is Love.

When God created man he created him happy. Now that we are fallen in our sin, God has committed the care and restoration of our souls to no less a person than the eternal Son of his love. Christ is the Captain of our salvation. What enemy is too strong for us when we are fighting under his banner? Did not the Son of God come down from heaven and live among us so that he might recover the life of God for us and restore the image of God in us?

Secondly, consider the work of God's Son. All of Christ's mighty works and painful suffering was endured for our salvation. For this salvation Christ laboured and worked. For this salvation he bled and died. After going through the pain of childbirth has he brought forth nothing but emptiness? Has he brought no deliverance to this earth? Will he not see the fruit of his labour?

It is absolutely impossible to believe that this great plan of salvation could have failed. Besides, we know that it has already been effective in saving many millions of people. And they were as far from the kingdom of God as we imagine ourselves to be right now.

Our High Priest 'continues forever... [and] is also able to save to the uttermost those who come to God through Him' (Hebrews 7:24-25). Christ is tender and kind. He knows our troubles and has gone through our temptations. Remember, 'a bruised reed He will not break and smoking flax He will not quench' (Isaiah 42:3).

Thirdly, God has sent forth his Holy Spirit. The Spirit's gentle but powerful wind is still blowing everywhere in the world. He is quickening and reviving people. He is waking people to their true purpose by helping them to know God. He is ready to assist weak, struggling people like us as we strive towards holiness. Once the Spirit has captured a soul and has lit a fire of God's love he will protect it. He will blow upon it and fan it into a burning flame of passion which 'many waters cannot quench' (Song of Songs 8:7).

Whenever the day begins to dawn and 'the morning star arises in your hearts' (2 Peter 1:19) it will easily dispel the devil's darkness. He will make all the ignorance, folly, selfishness, and sin flee as fast as the darkest night when the sun bursts over the horizon. For, 'the path of the just is as the shining light, that shineth more and more unto the perfect day' (Proverbs 4:18, AV). 'They go from strength to strength' (Psalm 84:7) until every one of them appears before God in Zion.

Why do we think it is impossible for real goodness and love to rule our hearts? Didn't God create us with a nature capable of love and goodness? Sin and evil are intruders. Even though they have held men captive for so long, 'from the beginning it was not so' (Matthew 19:8). Selfishness, which most people think is a part of our nature, is really a foreign invader and has no place in man's original innocence.

All of us know that we ought to love our Creator. We know that we should love him with our whole heart. The truth is our wills would do just that if they hadn't been corrupted by sin. But isn't the One who created our souls able to heal and restore them again? Can't we, by God's power, conquer the enemies of our souls?

As soon as we take up arms in this holy war we will have all the saints on earth and the angels of heaven on our side. The church throughout the world is daily praying to God for the success of all such effort. Without a doubt, the angels of heaven are deeply concerned about us and desire to see the life of God prevail in this world. They want the will of God to be done by us on earth like it is by them in heaven. We should encourage ourselves the same way the prophet did his servant. He showed him the chariots of fire and said, 'Fear not, for they that be with us are more than they that be with them [the Syrians]' (2 Kings 6:16, AV).

2. Trusting God and taking action

Reject any fear and despair that you might be feeling! Working hard to change *and* trusting God for help is more than half the battle. 'Arise and begin working and the LORD will be with you' (1 Chronicles 22:16). The salvation of a person's soul is the direct work of God and all of our human effort cannot produce it. We cannot earn the power that is necessary to save us. The Holy Spirit must come upon us and the power of God must overshadow us before we can be born again.

But we must not expect that this will happen without any action on our part. We must not lie in the ditch waiting until God pulls us out of it. No! No! We must apply ourselves to our fullest ability and only then can we have hope that 'our labour will not be in vain in the Lord' (1 Corinthians 15:58).

All the skill and hard work of man cannot create the smallest herb or make a stalk of corn grow. It is the energy of nature and the power of God that produces these things. It is God who causes the grass to grow. Still, no one will try to argue that the labours of men are unnecessary. In the same way, the human soul was created by God. He forms it and gives it life. Yet, God has appointed the marriage bed as the natural way to propagate the human race.

God must intervene with his power to change the soul of man, but we ought to do what we can to prepare ourselves. We must break up our fallow ground, root out the weeds, and pull up the thorns so that we will be ready to receive the seeds of grace and the rain from heaven. It is true that God has been found by some who did not seek him. Some people have been stopped in their tracks and captured by God. This is how Paul was converted on his journey to Damascus.

But this is not God's usual method of saving men. God has not limited himself to certain means he uses to save men, but he has tied us to them. We never have more reason to expect God's help than when we are making our most intense efforts.

3. The steps we ought to take

Therefore, next I will explain the steps we should take to receive the spirit I have been describing. If these ideas differ from what others have to say don't think I am contradicting or opposing them. Doctors often prescribe different treatments for the same disease. No one should pretend that only his method can bring a cure.

It has caused a great deal of unnecessary turmoil to some godly people that their experience is not exactly what they have read about in some books. God has different ways of dealing with men's souls. It is sufficient that the work is accomplished no matter what means are used.

Although I must follow a logical order in giving you these instructions, I do not mean to suggest that a person has to follow these steps in exact order. The directions I am giving work together and should be followed only as one is able to carry them out.

We must repent of all sin

I will not hold you back any longer. If we desire to have our souls changed and become like Christ we must seriously resolve to avoid and abandon all sinful practices. There can be no peace with God until we lay down our weapons of rebellion that we use to fight against him. We cannot expect to have our disease cured if we feed on poison every day.

Every sin wounds our soul and moves us further away from God. Our hearts will never be purified until we cleanse our hands from wickedness. We cannot excuse ourselves by pretending godliness is impossible to achieve. Our outward man is in some way in our own power. Just as we control our hands and tongue, we have some control over our thoughts and imagination as well. We have at least enough control to divert ourselves from sinful objects and to turn our minds in a better direction.

I admit that our sinful nature is very powerful. We have so many temptations that it requires a great deal of resolve and care to keep ourselves pure even in the smallest degree. But our power of self-control grows stronger as we make the effort to practice it.

We must know what sin is

To overcome our drive to sin we must learn what sin is. We must not take our values from the world or even from the practices of good men. Most people have very little under-standing of the real nature of sin. They are unaware of personal faults unless they are flagrant and shameful. Men rarely consider anything to be sin except what they define as extreme. Even the most sincere people often allow them-selves too much liberty and freedom in judging themselves. We forget how much pride, folly and sin is displayed in our everyday actions and words. Even if we are humbled by our sin and are fighting against it and gaining ground every day, our progress is so slow and our failures are so many that we need a better pattern to follow.

Every one of us is personally responsible for our sins. The actions of others will never excuse us. It is foolishness to determine what we will do by any other standard than the one by which we will be judged. If we would ever 'cleanse [our] way' it will be by 'taking heed' to God's Word (Psalm 119:9). His Word is 'living and powerful, and sharper than any two-edged sword, piercing even to the division of soul and spirit ... and is a discerner of the thoughts and intents of the heart' (Hebrews 4:12). It will reveal to us as sinful many things that the world considers completely innocent.

Therefore, we should imitate the psalmist who said, 'concerning the works of men, by the word of Your lips I have kept away from the paths of the destroyer' (Psalm 17:4). We should fully learn the truths of our faith. By thoughtfully studying the words of Christ (especially the Sermon on the Mount in Matthew chapters 5 to 7) and the teachings of the apostles we can learn what is expected of us.

We should never consider any sin small or unimportant. The smallest sin is both infinitely terrible in the sight of God and harmful to our souls. If we truly understood sin we would be as deeply burdened by the smallest sin as we are by the worst of crimes.

We must think about the consequences of sin

Some sins are powerfully attached to us. Sometimes slavery to a particular sin is a product of our nature. Sometimes it is because we have allowed it to become a habit. In some people the pleasure that sin gives them is the root of its hold on them. Forsaking some sins will be like cutting off a hand or plucking out an eye. But that must not lead us to wait until it is easy and all temptation has ceased before we repent of our sins.

We must not imitate the foolish poet who stood by the river all day waiting for all the water to pass by. We must not indulge our sinful desires like little children, until we grow tired of the sin of which we are unwilling to let go. We cannot continue in a sin, and at the same time hope that God's grace will one day overpower our spirits and make us hate that sin.

Even if (supposing the worst) we are destitute of spiritual life and any ability to discern what is evil, and even if we honestly do not hate sin, we still have enough common sense to realize how harmful sin is to us. Often that alone can persuade us to change our lives. Even if knowing the serious spiritual effects of sin cannot change us, the fear of sin's awful consequences might. The same selfish spirit that makes us pursue sinful pleasures will make us unwilling to sin when the cost of sin is too high. In a way we can use our selfish nature against itself and use one natural desire to defeat another.

For this reason, we should make it a habit to think about what a fearful thing it is to anger and offend God. After all, we depend on him every moment. If he withdraws his mercy we will be miserable. If he removes his help we will be nothing.

It would also help us to remember the brevity and uncertainty of life. We only have a few days in this world. It is just a short time before we all go down into the dark and silent grave. If we continue in sin we will take nothing with us when we die except anguish and regret.

Think of the horror that must overwhelm the unforgiven soul who finds himself standing all alone before the all-knowing and just Judge of the world. There he will have to give an account for his whole life, even down to the smallest details. Every word the tongue has spoken and every secret thought that ever passed through the mind will be judged.

We should also think about the terror of that day when the foundations of the earth will be shaken. The heavens will pass away with a great noise and the elements will melt with a fervent heat (see 2 Peter 3:10) and this present world will be destroyed. Jesus came humbly into this world to purchase salvation for us and to plead with us to accept this gift. Soon he will appear the second time. But this time he will come in the full majesty of his glory. He will descend from heaven in flaming fire to take vengeance on those who have despised his mercy and continued in their rebellion against him (see 2 Thessalonians 1:7-9).

At that time all the hidden things of darkness will be made manifest. Our secret sins that others never suspected us of will be exposed and laid open to public view. Thousands of actions that we never dreamed were sinful and things we had completely forgotten about will be laid upon our conscience. There will be such a powerful conviction of guilt that we will neither be able to deny nor excuse our sins.

At that time all the angels in heaven and all the saints who ever lived on earth will approve of the dreadful sentence that will be passed on wicked men. Even people whom they may have loved and admired on earth will be looked on with disgust and wrath. They will not make one prayer for their deliverance for their judgment is just.

We should also think about the eternal punishment that awaits the souls of the damned. Scripture uses pictures of the most terrible and painful things in this world to describe hell. But even these pictures are not sufficient to fully teach us the reality of hell. If we joined together all of the descriptions the Scriptures give us of hell and added to them all the misery and torment we could imagine they would still come short of the horror of what hell is really like.

I know that this is a sad, depressing subject. There is a great deal of anguish and horror just thinking about it. But how much more horrible it must be to have to endure it! Thinking about hell may frighten us enough to keep us from walking down the path that would lead us there. However fond we are of our sin, the fear of hell may make us forsake it. Our strongest temptations may be shaken and defeated when we are asked the question, 'who among us shall dwell with everlasting burnings?' (Isaiah 33:14).

This is the reason the Bible speaks of hell with words that are likely to influence a carnal mind. These fears will never be enough to make anyone truly good, but they might keep us from many evils and they have many times prepared the way for deep, lasting change.

We must diligently guard our souls

It is not enough just to think about these things once or twice. Nor is it enough to make a resolution to forsake our sins. We must maintain a constant guard and continual watch over our souls. Sometimes our heart is awakened to see the horrible consequences of a sinful life and immediately we resolve to change. But so often we quickly fall asleep again and we lose the hope we had of victory over these sins. It is then that temptation takes advantage of us. Sin is always calling on us. It seduces us and often gains our consent before we are aware of what is happening.

It is the folly and ruin of many people to live carelessly. They take part in everything that comes their way without ever thinking about what they are about to do or say. If our resolutions are going to be effective we must take heed to our ways. We must watch our words. We must guard our hearts. We must demand that our heart tells us where it is leading us. We need to know if pride, passion or wickedness is motivating our actions. We must consider whether or not God will be offended by our actions or if anyone will be offended by them. If we do not have the time for deep reflection, we ought to at least turn our eyes toward God, put ourselves in his presence and ask him for permission and approval for what we are about to do.

We must often examine our actions

Careful attention to our actions should be followed by regular, serious reflection on them. This will lead us to repentance, confession and forgiveness. But it will also help us to reinforce and strengthen our resolutions, and learn to resist and reject temptations that have previously defeated us. Even though it was not a Christian who first suggested it, it is good advice to review and examine all the activities

67

of a day before we go to sleep at night. This will give us comfort for what we have done right and correction for what we have done wrong. It will also turn the shipwrecks of one day into markers directing our voyage the next day. This could even be called the art of godly living. This practice would contribute greatly to our growth in holiness.

As we fight against sin we must not forget to seek God's help. This is especially necessary as we fight against those sins that so easily trip us up. I think that even if we have not yet become new creatures God will hear our cries for help. Our God hears the cry of the birds. So surely he will listen to the prayers that come from the desires that he himself has planted in our hearts. What I have already said about the consequences of sin ought to make us plead with God about sin as earnestly as we do about life's other difficulties. If nothing else, prayers against sin will be powerful weapons to inspire us to be cautious. We are likely to be ashamed to keep committing the same sins we have just asked God to help us fight against.

We must show restraint even in lawful things

We can make the first steps toward the life of God by restraining our natural desires. This will keep them from becoming sinful habits. Christian wisdom will teach us to abstain from pleasures that are not unlawful. This will not only help us grow in holiness, it will also help us weaken the strength of our sinful nature. It will teach our appetites to obey us. We need to treat our souls as wise parents treat their children. Parents often make their children obey them in small, unimportant matters so that they will become submissive. Then they will obey when it comes to the important issues of life.

So the person who wants to put to death his pride should not even listen to the praise he deserves. In some cases he should not try to clear himself when he has been unjustly criticized. This is especially true if the criticism only reflects on his wisdom and not on his conduct or virtue. In the same way, a person who is trying to control a hateful spirit would be wise to deny himself the satisfaction of telling other people when someone has hurt him. If we want to control our tongue we must get used to silence and solitude. Sometimes, like the psalmist, we should hold '[our] peace even from good' (Psalm 39:2) until we have gained some control over our tongue. We can restrain our natural reactions and control our desires by getting them used to being denied. Even so, we must go further. It is not enough just to have them under control.

We must resist loving the world

Our next effort must be to wean our hearts from the materialism and pleasures of this world. These drag us down and depress our souls and retard our growth toward God. We can wean ourselves if we become persuaded of the emptiness of worldly pleasures.

This is a common subject and everyone talks about it. But very few really believe what they say. Ideas float around in our heads and slide off of our tongues, but the truth we pretend to believe has not captured our hearts. We know that all the glory and pleasures of this world are empty and

69

yet they still occupy all of our thoughts, enslave our hearts, keep us from better things, and lead us into many sins. Sometimes we get serious about living for God and ignore the things of the world and resolve not to be deceived by them anymore. But this mood seldom outlives the next temptation. The things we shut out at the front door get back in through the window.

Sin still makes claims and promises which deceive us. Even after we have been frustrated by the empty promises of this world a thousand times we still seem compelled to keep repeating the same mistakes. The slightest difference in circumstances tricks us into thinking we shall find real satisfaction and true joy in sin, even though this has never happened before. If somehow we could become truly free from this world, and develop a real hatred for its fleeting pleasures, we would have taken a giant step forward in our spiritual journey.

The soul of man, however, has a raging thirst that cannot be extinguished. There is an invisible fire that is always grasping for something to satisfy its longings. It is always on a quest for what will make it happy. If our hearts could somehow be completely torn away from this world and its pleasures, they would at once begin to search for some higher, more noble object to satisfy their burning passionate desires. If they were no longer blinded by the empty glories of this world they would fix their gaze on God. In him they would discover the beauty and joy that satisfies their deepest yearnings. God could then be the object of man's deepest love and devotion.

Love for this world and love for God are like the scales of a balance. As one of them falls the other rises. When the things of this world are exalted in our hearts, faith becomes weak and begins to decline. But when they lose their beauty and begin to wither away, our hearts gain composure and stop seeking them. It is then that the seeds of grace take root in our hearts, and the life of God begins to flourish and prevail in our souls.

Because of this it is vital for us to realize how empty and vain the pleasures of this world are. We must persuade our hearts to fall out of love with the things of this world. To carry this out we must take into account everything that common sense, faith, our own experiences and the experiences of others can teach us about the vanity of the pleasures of this world. We must meditate on this over and over again and focus our thoughts on this truth until we become fully persuaded.

We need to stop all of our pursuits and plans and ask ourselves why we are doing all these things? What is our goal? Do we really think that wealth, fame or sin can satisfy our soul? Have we not already tried these things? Are they going to produce a greater joy or more contentment tomorrow than they did yesterday? Will they make us happier next year than we were last year?

There might be a difference between what you are pursuing now and what you pursued previously. But the things you pursued previously looked every bit as promising before you had them as the things you are going after now. Like a rainbow they looked glorious from a distance, but when you got close you found them to be only emptiness and vapour. Man's life would be barren if he were not capable of anything higher.

We must develop disciplines

When our desires for worldly things are somewhat subdued we must develop disciplines that will stir up and awaken the life of God. First, we should sincerely try to carry out the duties that the Christian faith requires of us, and the things we would want to do if Christ's life ruled our hearts. If we can't change our souls now, we should at least seek to control our outward behaviour. Even if our hearts are not burning with the love of God, we should still be devoted to him, by attending church, listening to his Word, offering him praise, and encouraging others to serve him. Even if we lack the love and compassion that we ought to have for others, we should still not neglect any chance to do good things for them. Even if our hearts are full of pride and arrogance, we must still work at being modest and humble.

These external performances of duty are of very little value in themselves, but they may help us progress toward better things. It is true that Paul said, 'bodily exercise profits a little' (1 Timothy 4:8) but he did not say that it is totally useless. It is always good to be doing what we can. For it is then that God is likely to pity our weakness and assist our feeble efforts.

These efforts are also important because they will make it much easier for us to live the Christian life when true love and humility take root in our hearts. We do not need to fear the charge of hypocrisy. Even if our actions outrun our affections they still come from a knowledge of our duty, and our desire is not to appear better than we are, but to become what we ought to be.

We must try to develop love for God

Acts that come from the heart have a more direct influence on the soul. These acts shape the soul into what it ought to be. Therefore, there are things we should often practice. If we cannot say that we love God with our whole heart, we should at least confess that we should do so and that it would be our joy to do so.

The dishonour that is done to the name of God by sinful men ought to break our hearts. At the same time, we ought to applaud the praise and worship he receives from the angels and saints in heaven.

We should always be submitting ourselves to God's laws and will. Even if our stubborn hearts jump back from him in rebellion, we should still confess that his will is always just and good. Since this is true, we should be willing to allow him to do with us whatever he pleases whether we like it or not.

As for developing in us love for all men, we must frequently pray for the happiness of everyone we know. When we give gifts to the poor we should follow these up with sincere prayers that God would take care of them and deliver them out of all their distress.

Doing these things will be the path toward godliness. When we use the powers we have the Spirit of God is likely to join in and raise our deeds to a higher level and give them the imprint of God. Once we have often and repeatedly done these things we will discover that we are able to do them with more freedom and ease.

4. Meditation is a powerful tool

I will only mention two other means for developing holiness and godliness. The first is thinking deeply and seriously about the importance and truth of the Christian faith. The thought most people give to the truth of God is pretty weak and ineffective. We see the proof of this careless thinking in the tendency that some people have to blindly follow the Christian faith simply because it is in fashion. The fact is people like that really do not care if these things are true or not.

People generally do not want to disagree with the religion of their culture. So if their neighbours are Christian they are content to call themselves Christians as well. But they seldom make any effort to think about the evidence for the truth and they do not stop to consider what it means to their lives. That is why their behaviour is not changed by their faith. One person correctly said that this kind of faith is 'without spirit and unable to move anyone'. A thoughtless faith cannot move a person's will or change his heart.

Therefore, we have to develop true belief and full conviction about God's truth. Our thoughts must dwell on his truth until we are convinced it is right and until it changes our hearts. We need to urge our spirits forward into the spiritual world and fix our minds on things above. This must be done until we clearly see that these things are not a fantasy and that everything else is but a dream and a shadow.

When we look around us and see the beauty, wonder, order and harmony of creation our thoughts should be lifted towards the Creator who made everything and upholds it all by his power and goodness. When we consider mankind we need to see that we are not just a piece of organized matter or a strange but well-designed engine. There is more to us than flesh and blood. There is in us the capacity to know, love and enjoy our Creator. Even though the soul is now burdened with sinful flesh, before long it will be freed and will live without the body.

We can also lift our thoughts from this earth with all of its folly, sin and misery and raise them toward heaven with all of its glory. There the saints and angels live eternally in God's presence and know no other emotions than joy and love. Then, we can think about how the Son of God left that beautiful world to come to this earth, to live and die so that he could bring to us that same joy that is experienced by those in heaven. Consider how he overcame the pain of death and opened the kingdom of heaven to all who believe. He has sat down on the right hand of the Majesty on high and even now is praying for us. Every day he sends the power of his Spirit upon his church. It is like the sun reaching us with beams of light and warmth.

We must think about the excellence of God

Thinking seriously and frequently about God's truth is the best way of producing a living faith. That living faith is the foundation of Christianity and the root of the life of God in the soul of man. Let me then suggest some particular subjects for meditation that will produce the fruits of the life of God.

First, to inflame our hearts with the love of God we should think about the greatness of God's glory and his love for us. We know very little about God's glory, but what we do know is enough to fill our souls with wonder and love. We are not merely creatures with physical senses. That would make it impossible to love anything except what we can see with our eyes.

We all know that someone we have never seen can capture our hearts. Why are we captivated by these people? It is not because of the colour of their skin or external beauty. If that were all that attracted us we would fall in love with statues and pictures and flowers. Physical beauty is pleasing to the eye, but it would never prevail on our hearts if it didn't represent some real glory. We love them because we see in them some spiritual strength or wisdom and goodness. It is their character that charms us and causes us to love them. These things are not seen by the physical eyes. Our eyes can only see the outward effects these characteristics have on a person.

If the unseen attributes of a man can capture our love, then surely the beauty of God's nature could lure our hearts if we ever seriously thought about it. God's goodness and wisdom fill the universe. His glory is displayed in every corner of creation. Shouldn't we be more moved by his glory than we often seem to be by the faint reflection of this glory that we see in our fellow man? Should we love the scattered pieces of a crude, imperfect picture and never be affected by the beauty of the original? This would be stupid blindness that would defy explanation!

Whatever beauty we see in another person should not hold our affections. Instead it ought to lift our hearts to God in love. We should come to the conclusion that if there is so much sweetness in a drop there must be so much more in the fountain. If there is so much splendour in a ray, what must the sun be in all of its glory?

We cannot use the excuse that God is too remote, as if he were too far away to hear us or receive our love. 'He is not far from each one of us, for in Him we live and move and have our being' (Acts 17:27-8). We cannot open our eyes without seeing some traces of his glory. We cannot turn our eyes toward him without seeing that he is pursuing us and waiting for us to look to him to bring us into fellowship with himself.

Therefore, we must raise our thoughts to think clearly about God's nature and glory. We need to consider all that his works declare about him and all that his Word reveals of him. We should especially think about the revelation of God to us in his Son. He is the 'brightness of His glory and the express image of His person' (Hebrews 1:3). Jesus Christ came into this world and revealed both what God is like and what we are meant to be.

When we read about the life of Christ in the Gospels we see the glory of God veiled in human flesh. It is in the Gospels we can see the clearest picture of a man with unlimited power, wisdom and goodness. There we look upon him who is the author and fountain of all glory. We should fix the eyes of our soul upon him. When we do our eyes may touch our hearts, and while we are musing the fire will burn within us (see Psalm 39:3).

We must think about the love of God

We ought to make a special effort to meditate on how good God is to us. Knowing that we are loved by him is sure to win our heart's affection. Whenever someone speaks affectionately to us it always seems to please us. This is true even if the one who expresses love is otherwise unbecoming. Therefore, to know that the God of heaven loves and cares for us has to delight the heart. His love will capture our spirits, melt our hearts, and ignite our whole souls into a flame of devotion.

Not only does the Bible tell us that God loves us, all the works of God also loudly proclaim his love. God gives us life and he renews that gift with every breath we take. He has placed us in a world that has everything we need. He sends down blessings from heaven and he causes the earth to bring forth our food. He gives us clothing and shelter. While we use the provisions of one year he is preparing more for the next year. He gives us many comforts and

78

pleasures that make life sweet. God's eye is always on us and he cares about our needs. He watches over us even when we are sound asleep and unaware of his presence.

Someone might be tempted to think that these gifts really do not prove God's love since he can grant these things without much trouble. But before you believe that you should remember that God has acted in a way that clearly shows how much he cares for us. God has proven his love in his suffering for us. Since God cannot suffer in his own nature he took our nature. The eternal Son of God left heaven and the praise of the angels behind to clothe himself in human flesh so that he could dwell among men. He came to this world and wrestled with the stubbornness and rebellion of the human race. He showed humanity the folly of its own way and then offered us a new and living way by dying for our sins.

I remember that a poet had a creative way of describing how this love of God had attracted him after a long period of resistance. He said the God of love had shot all of his golden arrows at him but could never pierce his heart. Finally, God put himself on the bow and shot himself like an arrow into the poet's breast. I think that this does, in a way, picture God's method of dealing with us. For a long time God wrestled with a stubborn world. He had sent down many blessings upon it. When none of his other gifts could overcome our rebellion, God made a gift of himself. This gift proves the greatness of his love and wins the hearts of men.

The Gospels are the story of Christ's love for us. All the pain and trouble he endured were the fruit and proof of his love. But the greatest proof was the last scene of his life. Is it possible to remember the cross and question his love for us or deny him our love? It is on the cross that we should fix our most serious attention. Then 'Christ may dwell in your hearts by faith; that you, being rooted and grounded in love, may be able to comprehend with all the saints what is the breadth and length and depth and height – to know the love of Christ which passes all knowledge…'(Ephesians 3:17-19).

Do not also forget all the acts of grace and love that God has shown us. Remember how long he has put up with our foolish actions and sins. God was gracious to us while he patiently wrestled with our stubborn hearts. He has used every possible means to reclaim us for himself.

Have you considered all of the blessings God has given you and how many times he has delivered you from trouble? Some of these blessings were given in ways that clearly prove they were not just chance happenings. These blessings were plainly given by God's gracious hand and they were in answer to prayer.

I also hope that we do not accept the silly idea that God does these things in order to increase our guilt and make our punishment more severe. God is love and he takes no pleasure in the destruction of his creatures. If we abuse his goodness and turn his grace into a chance to sin, that is our fault and not his. If we plunge ourselves deeper into guilt it is because of the hardness of our own hearts. God does not

80

desire that we should use his gifts to increase our own guilt. That is our doing.

If we would take to heart what I have written about God's greatness and love, it would bring forth love in our hearts for God. As a result we would be more easily led into the other fruits of the life of God in the soul of man. Since that is true I will not need to write as much about those things.

We should learn to love others

We will learn to love other people more if we stop to consider that they are God's creatures and are made in his image. Every person is the workmanship of God's own hand. God has a very special love and care for them. He planned a way for them to be happy before the foundation of the world. God is willing to live with them in close fellowship through all of eternity.

The worst person we can think of is still the offspring of heaven and one of the children of the Most High. However wickedly a person acts, as long as God has not disowned him by the final judgment, he would want us to treat him as one of his creatures. He would want us to embrace him with a sincere and friendly affection.

You know that we naturally care about the family of the people we love. We gladly try to make the child of a friend happy. In the same way, if we truly love God we should try to love his children. If for no other reason, we should love them because God does. Every soul is more precious to God than all the wealth of this world. They are so precious that

God did not think the blood of his only Son too high a price for their salvation. So should we not treat them as precious too?

Since everyone is created by God, they have his image stamped on them. Therefore, we are obliged to love them. In some people God's image is more obvious and we can easily see the beauty of God's wisdom and goodness in them. In other people God's image is distorted and marred by sin. But it is not completely destroyed and some traces of it still remain. All people are given rational, immortal souls. Everyone has a mind and a will that is capable of great things. If they are disordered and out of order because of sin, it should cause us to pity them and not hate them.

It is hard to love someone who is mean, foolish, and proud or who uses foul language. It would help us to think of these things as diseases of the soul. The soul of the wicked person is capable of the same wisdom and goodness as the best of saints. It has the potential to be raised to a level of glory that would make it fit for heaven. If we could see this it would turn our dislike into sympathy. This attitude would help us look at the sinful soul with the same feelings we have for someone with a body that has been disfigured by some awful disease. Even though we hate the sin we still need to love the sinner.

Knowing our dignity will help us develop purity

Thinking about the dignity of our nature will help to free us of the love of this world and its sinful pleasures. Man is a noble creature made in the image of God. Because of that it is disgraceful for us to wallow in sin. Man was made for higher things. The things of this world only steal our true joy and pleasure.

We should not be feeding and babying the beast in us and starving the spirit. If we could only realize what we are and why we were created we would have the right kind of self-respect. Knowing ourselves in this way would create in us a true modesty and holy humility. We would become very careful about participating in even the smallest of worldly pleasures.

Think about the joys of heaven

Thinking about heaven and the joy that awaits us there has a great benefit. In heaven are 'pleasures for forevermore' (Psalm 16:11). The power of this kind of meditation is spoken of in the Bible: 'Every one who has this hope in Him, purifies himself just as He is pure' (1 John 3:3). If our eternal home is always in our thoughts we will truly become like 'sojourners and pilgrims, [abstaining] from fleshly lusts which war against the soul' (1 Peter 2:11). Such thoughts of heaven will help to keep us 'unspotted from the world' (James 1:27), and prepare us for the pleasures and joy of heaven.

We need to make sure our thoughts of heaven are not earthly and carnal. The pictures used to describe heaven should not be the only thoughts we have of that place and all its joy. If that is the only way we think of it, it could have a bad effect on us by further trapping us in carnal affections. As a result we might start indulging ourselves in

83

what we think is a foretaste of heaven. We need to see that heaven's pleasures are holy and spiritual. Then, when our minds are filled with true thoughts of heaven's joys, everything here below will become empty in our eyes. When this happens we will reject pleasures that would rob us of heaven's joy or in any way make us unfit to receive them.

Humility

The last fruit of the life of God to be considered is humility. We never lack material to think about that will produce humility in us. All of our wickedness, foolishness and sin should help to cast down any proud thoughts we had about ourselves. Other people respect us because they see some small good in us. But they do not know about the many evils that are in us. If they really knew us they would quickly change their opinion. If the thoughts that pass through our minds on our best day were exposed to public view we would either be hated or mocked.

Even if we are able to hide our failures from each other we are still aware of them ourselves. Some serious thought about them would greatly diminish and subdue any pride that is in our hearts. The people who are most holy usually think worse of themselves than they do of other people. This is not because their sins are worse than the sins of other people. Instead, it is because they are more aware of their own failures than the failures of others. They realize all the pain their sins have caused. But when they consider other people's faults they only want to help do away with their pain.

One writer made a good point when he said that the deepest humility is not produced by thinking about our failures. We become most humble when we think about God's purity and holiness. The stains on our lives are clearly seen when we are in the light of his presence. We are never less in our own eyes as we are when we see ourselves through God's eyes. Oh how weak our holiness looks when we see him. The humility that is produced by seeing our own sin is harsh. But the humility that is produced by seeing God's glory is not as harsh.

5. Prayer will draw us close to God

Fervent, heartfelt prayer is another discipline that will help bring about a holy change. Holiness is a gift of God. Indeed, it is the greatest gift we can receive from him. God committed himself to giving us this gift when he promised his Holy Spirit to those who ask. When we pray we approach God's presence and we are open to his influence. In prayer the Son of righteousness blesses us with the rays of his glory. And the light of his glory chases away the darkness of our sin and burns his image on our soul.

There is no need to go into great detail about the ways to pray and the benefits of prayer. Many books have been written on this subject. Instead, I will tell you that just as there is prayer in which we make use of our voice, there is, secondly, a kind of prayer in which we utter no sound. In this kind of prayer we form the words in our minds and conceive of the expressions in our hearts.

There is a third kind of prayer in which we neither speak nor think words. There are times after we have thought long and hard about God that our hearts rise to him and all we can do is sigh and groan. There are some thoughts that are too deep for words. After deep thoughts about the glory of God a person might find himself unable to express to God how great his majesty is and how much he adores him. Or after heart-breaking thoughts about one's own sin and failure a person might fall down before him with shame and sorrow, not even lifting his eyes toward heaven nor daring to speak even one word. Or when a person has deeply considered the beauty of holiness and the joy of saints, he might long for God in prayers words cannot express. He might even continue repeating this as long as he is upheld by God's Spirit.

This kind of prayer is the most effective prayer for purifying our souls and helping them to grow in holiness. It could even be called the great secret of devotion. This may be what Paul had in mind when he said, 'The Spirit ... helps us in our weaknesses ... making intercession for us with groanings that cannot be uttered' (Romans 8:26). Or as it could be translated, 'with groaning that cannot be worded'.

This kind of prayer should not replace the other kinds of prayer. We have many things for which to pray and prayers of this kind require so much time and effort that it is not easy to do this all of the time. Also, these deep sighs of the heart are likely to be difficult for us. This makes it hard to do this all the time. But certainly some time spent in seriously pursuing a few of these inward prayers will do much for our souls.

86

6. The Lord's Supper helps our progress

My dear friend, I have briefly proposed the ways I think are helpful to bring about lasting change in our souls. The same means which help create the life must be used in order to strengthen our souls and help them to grow. Now, I want to recommend one more discipline for that purpose – the frequent use of the Lord's Supper.

Communion (another name for the Supper) has been given to us to nurture spiritual life once it has been birthed in the soul. All the disciplines of the Christian life meet together at the Lord's Table. There we put into practice all of the other disciplines I have already mentioned.

While partaking of the Lord's Supper we place strict requirements on ourselves, we raise our thoughts to heaven and feel contempt for the things of this world. Every grace works in us with power and strength. All of the subjects I recommend for meditation present themselves to us in the communion meal. Because of this it has great profit for us. It is while we partake of the Lord's Supper that we make our greatest advance toward heaven. But the neglect of, or careless participation in, the Supper is one of the main obstacles to spiritual growth.

It is time to close this letter. It has grown to a far greater length than I had expected. If these suggestions can do you even the slightest good, I will be very happy. I am hoping that you will accept my efforts. I am indebted to you for all you have done for me.

7. Closing prayer

Oh, most gracious God the Father and fountain of mercy and goodness, you have blessed us by showing us how happy we can be and then showing us the way that leads to that happiness. Awaken in our souls such a strong desire for this joy that we will pursue it with all our hearts. Do not let us trust in our own strength and neither let us doubt your help. While we are making our greatest effort, teach us to depend upon you for success.

Open our eyes and teach us out of your law. Bless us with clear, heartfelt knowledge of our duty and a mind that can discern what is evil. Oh that our ways were directed to keep your statutes. Then we would not be ashamed for we would respect all your commandments.

Fill our hearts with a holy hatred for the empty pleasures this world tempts us with. Grant that these pleasures will never be able to seduce us and betray us to any sin. Turn our eyes away from looking at the vain things of this world and make us alive to your law.

Fill our souls with a deep understanding of the great truths you have revealed in the gospel. Let these truths influence our lives in such a way that they guide our every step. May the life we live here in the flesh be lived by faith in the Son of God.

Oh that the glory of your goodness and love would conquer our hearts so that they would be always rising to you in flames of love and growing in love toward all men for your sake. Cleanse us from all filthiness of flesh and spirit. May we grow in holiness, without which we can never hope to see and enjoy you.

Finally, O God, grant that our thoughts of you and our knowledge of ourselves would humble us before you and stir up strong desires for you. We desire to submit ourselves to the guidance of your Holy Spirit. Lead us in your truth and teach us, for you are the God of our salvation. Guide us with your counsel and afterward receive us into glory because of the works and prayers of your blessed Son our Saviour. Amen.

PART 2

How to nurture abundant life

Robert Leighton

How to nurture abundant life

Dear Friend,

I am writing to you in the hope that I might help you grow toward spiritual maturity. I am going to recommend some spiritual exercises and practices that will help your Christian growth. These disciplines are useful in nurturing the life of God in the soul of man. The Christian who practices these is like the farmer who prepares his fields and plants seed in them. He works hard and does what he can and must do for his fields to be fruitful. Still, the good farmer knows that the harvest depends upon the favour of God in sending the rain and sunshine at the right time.

For the life of God to grow in your soul you must 'exercise yourself … to godliness' (1 Timothy 4:7). But God must rain his mercy upon you also. Your heart must be touched by his holy goodness before you can hope to see the fruit of spiritual maturity produced in you. So, you 'must work out your own salvation with fear and trembling' (Philippians 2:12), but you also must trust in the wonderful mercy of God with all of your heart.

Even though it is not possible to be perfect in this life, we can grow to great heights of spiritual maturity. The life of God, by its very nature, must always be growing and moving us closer to the perfection we see in Jesus. Why do some people become more like Jesus than others? Surely, it is because they desire this with all their heart. If you will fervently, passionately, and continually long for, humbly pray for and diligently labour for Christlikeness, it will no doubt be given to you.

Do not think for one moment that doing spiritual exercises without passion or heart will transform your life or help you to grow. Spiritual disciplines in themselves have no power to change us. If, though, they are carried out as acts of passionate longing for holiness they are very valuable as a means of spiritual growth.

God is full of mercy and goodness, and when you diligently seek perfection he will bring about spiritual growth in your soul. I do not mean absolute perfection, for that is not attainable in this life. I mean the relative perfection of an increasing holiness of life. The spiritual exercises that I am going to recommend to you are ways of seeking after, asking for, and knocking on, the door of this holiness. So when you diligently seek holiness you will find it. When you fervently ask for holiness it will be given unto you. When you continually knock on the door of holiness it will be opened unto you.

I need, however, to warn you of some perils to avoid as you begin to practice spiritual disciplines. You might, for example, be tempted to abandon public worship in order to spend all of your time in private devotions. Nor should spiritual disciplines be used an excuse to avoid serving others. Our private spiritual exercises should actually lead us into public service. We should follow the pattern of the

Lord Jesus. He would spend time in quiet prayer and solitude and then engage in public ministry.

You should also be careful not to become too rigid in your spiritual disciplines. Some disciplines are helpful for a time, but subsequently you might well find that there are others that are more profitable. Be willing to change your practices as the Holy Spirit leads you, and make sure you apply to life what he teaches you in quiet times of spiritual reflection.

You will not always find pleasure in your devotions. Do not let this discourage you. Continue to be faithful, even when it is hard going and your heart is not in what you are doing. If you persevere for no other reason than to honour God, you will be rewarded for your effort.

Do not become disheartened by your failures. Do not allow your daily faults and imperfections to keep you from growing in the Lord. Be firm in your desire and effort to become more like the Lord Jesus. Always ask God for the best, aim for the best, and hope for the best. If you feel genuine sorrow that you cannot do better, your sorrow will be an acceptable sacrifice in the sight of God.

Always remember that 'in due season we shall reap if we not lose heart' (Galatians 6:9). Practice spiritual disciplines as much as you can but do not become legalistic about carrying them out. Your effort is not in vain if you are not able exactly and strictly to do them all. Continually seek to do better and by God's grace all will be well with you.

The discipline of meditating on God

Most gracious Lord, to know you is the very peace and joy of a man's soul. Yet, no one can know you unless you open their eyes and show yourself to them. So I humbly ask that in your infinite mercy you would enlighten my heart and mind to know you and your holy and perfect will, now and for evermore. I ask this to the honour and glory of your name. Amen.

The life of God in your soul will grow as you devote yourself to knowing God. One of the ways you can come to know God better is by deeply meditating on him. Of course, you must humbly agree that the Lord is excellent and glorious far beyond our ability to fully comprehend him. But you must still attempt to gain as much knowledge of the Lord as you can. By knowing God I do not just mean knowing about him. I mean that you should seek to know him personally. This involves study but it also involves seeking him in prayer. Knowing God in this way is a special gift he gives his children. Without question, it is the most precious gift we can receive.

So lift up your heart to God and meditate on his eternal and infinite power. Think often of his excellent wisdom, endless goodness, and amazing love. He is the only true God. He is most excellent, most high, and most glorious. He is everlasting and unchanging goodness, eternal and infinite love. God is so great that all the thoughts and words that are used to describe him are not sufficient even to express the smallest degree of his majesty.

Your heart can only know peace and rest when it rests in God. May this truth lead you to continually meditate on the blessed Trinity with devotion and faith. Worship the Father, Son and Holy Spirit with a meek and humble spirit. Think often of Jesus, the redeemer and lover of your soul. Faithfully walk with him in reverence, humility, obedience and submission.

You should also think long and hard about your own wretched condition. You, like every one else, have been defiled by sin and are guilty of wicked rebellion against God. All of our misery is due to our fall into sin. The only way you can ever experience true happiness is through faith-union with Jesus Christ.

When you think about yourself and others, let Jesus Christ be the standard by which you are measured. If you do this you will know that, compared to him, we are all less than nothing. But through this exercise you will find yourself learning to be content and even happy to be unknown in this world. Even if you were to become famous, you will be able to be at peace when others criticise or condemn you. Let me encourage you, though, as much as possible, not to allow such criticism to be justified by your foolish or sinful actions.

Make it your aim to hate sin and to feel great sorrow for your sins. I hope that you loathe yourself for having committed them. Once this sorrow takes hold of your heart do not stay there, but flee to Christ for the pardon that is in his precious blood.

Offer yourself to God through Jesus Christ as a sweet smelling sacrifice, and it will be acceptable in his sight. Give all that your have to him. Decide now to do everything and use everything for the honour and glory of God. Resolve that by God's grace you will use all of the strength of your body and soul in his service.

Most of all, my friend, meditate often on the death of Christ. Consider thoughtfully all that he suffered. Remember the beating, the whipping, and the mocking that he endured. Then, let your mind survey again the wondrous cross – his nail-pierced hands, the crown of thorns, the shame and contempt heaped upon him, the three hours of darkness and the incredible pain he endured. Then, remember he endured it all for your sake.

Jesus as Lord

Oh God let your light and love shine in my heart so that I may know and love you above all things, and live humbly before you. Allow me to be so enraptured by the wonder of your love that I am able to forget myself. May your love bind my heart so strongly to you that neither prosperity nor poverty is able to draw me away. Grant that I so delight in you that no suffering or trouble can cause me to stray from you. Let me come to know you so deeply that you become more real to me than I am to myself. Help me to be so aware of your holy presence that it always guides all my conduct. Allow me to live with the awareness of your everlasting love towards me. I am awed that you should love me as if I were the only creature you had to love. Who am I that you should love me so? Amen.

You must die to yourself before you can follow the humble crucified life of Jesus Christ. Before you became a Christian you set your mind on the sinful pleasures of this world. Now that you know Christ you must set your mind on the far better spiritual pleasures found in him. Before you can live this way, however, you must develop a spiritual way of seeing life.

You must commit yourself to the discipline of Jesus Christ. This means that you must always obey him without delay. In everything you need to seek his approval. What you say, what you do, and where you go, must be governed by the will of Jesus. To keep yourself on the right path you ought to ask yourself if you have walked in the will of God and followed the example of Christ. Even those things that you have to do because it is your duty to do them must be offered up to God through Christ. You should pray, 'Lord Jesus, keep me from every sin of mind and body by filling my heart with your blessed presence and wisdom.'

Be sure to bind your heart to Christ. Hold on to the cross and never depart from it. Live as one who is always in the presence of God. Commit everything to God's providence, knowing that he loves you and orders all things well. Believe with all your heart that he will bring sweetness out of every circumstance, right out of every wrong, and good out of every evil. If you have this faith you will bask in the light of the knowledge of the Lord.

Die to yourself and all things that keep you from loving God with your whole heart. Unite your soul so strongly to God that even if you must suffer on this earth you will be ready to do so by his grace if it is his will and brings glory to his name.

If you want God to be at home in your heart keep your mind pure and free from unholy thoughts. Do not allow wicked imaginations to dwell in you for they will rob you of the peace of his presence. Let your mind be decorated with portraits of Christ's holy life and death. Let holy thoughts so reign in your mind that the peace of God will always be with you.

Dying to self

Lord Jesus, everyday I fail. I find myself constantly tempted to sin. When I fall please pour out your grace so that I can rise again. Don't let me live arrogantly in silence after I sin. Instead, by your grace, bring me humbly before you to confess my sinfulness and wicked deeds. Push me forward into a repentance in which I am firmly resolved to change. Help me not to languish in hopeless despair, but instead grant to me faith to trust in your loving mercy and your readiness to forgive. Amen.

Discipline yourself totally to forsake everything that hinders your relationship with God. If something in your life dishonours God put it aside. Don't hold on to anything that is not God's will for your life. You will never be able fully to enjoy and appreciate the pleasures of God until you quit seeking pleasure by constantly giving in to your sinful lusts. If you possess anything that keeps you from Christ you must give it up and desire it no more for yourself or for anyone else.

We all tend to be self-centred. We can't seem to do anything, desire anything or even suffer anything without a selfish motive behind it all. We have this strange unnatural attachment that causes us to love God's gifts rather than God himself. This love of things always ends up with us falling into pride, gluttony, and greed. The only way to avoid this is for you to daily take up the cross and die to self.

You need to put to death all desire for things that tend to weaken your spiritual life. Even though some things we do are perfectly lawful, they can potentially defile the soul and grieve the Holy Spirit. For example, food is good and to be eaten with gratitude to God, but it can become a snare if you fall into gluttony. Therefore, you need to be careful about anything that might hinder your walk with God.

Loving God is a powerful weapon in helping us put to death the sinful desires that linger in our hearts. The best way to increase your love for God is by meditating on Christ. Try to imprint on your heart the very image of the crucified Lord. Think often of his holiness, meekness, kindness and humility. Your thoughts of him will develop into affection for him and your affection will blossom into love.

As you increasingly love God you will find that your soul will be purified. It is also vital for your spiritual growth and health that you live a life of love to God. When this life fills your heart it has a purifying effect. It helps to loosen your grip on the things of this world and strengthens your grasp on heavenly things.

One of the practical ways you can foster this kind of powerful spiritual life is by spending time in solitude and silence. This is very helpful in keeping you on the right path. Carry out your daily responsibilities without worrying. Keep your mind focused on God. Let love be the driving force of your actions.

This kind of spiritual life is impossible unless one dies to everything except God. A burning love for God will do more to produce love for others and a humble attitude toward yourself than anything else I can imagine. If our hearts have a pure love for God we will discover a grand spiritual freedom. The person who loves God with his whole heart always has God in mind.

One of the great barriers to spiritual growth is bitterness. You must put to death any bitterness that you might have towards any man. Also put to death all longing after recognition, honour and praise from others. As long as you hold on to this desire you will not be able to see your own unworthiness. Wanting the praise of others bars us from knowing God and enjoying him as the fountain of life, grace, and goodness.

Put to death also your love for the sweet experiences of grace that God gives to you. Such gifts of God are only meant to help us in our weakness, but in themselves they provide no real holiness. So we are not to put our trust even in such experiences. We must trust in Christ alone.

Put to death all excessive scruples of conscience. These often arise from our own inordinate self-love. They do no good, but disturb our peace, cast a dark cloud over our souls, and cool the fire of our love. Faith has the power to dispel the darkness that such scruples bring. Faith strengthens our confidence in God and creates a zeal for holiness. It works in our hearts to put to death ungodliness, and brings forth patience in adversity and gratitude in every circumstance.

Put to death impatience. When difficult circumstances arise, whether they are from God or men, put impatience to death. Put away all desire for revenge and do not allow resentment to fester in your heart. Love your enemies. Love them with the love of Christ. Love them as if they were your dearest friends.

All the sin and trouble we experience in this life are the fruits of self-centred living. Therefore, put to death your self-love and self-will, and in everything live for the will and pleasure of God. Be willing to suffer any trial, any pain, and any trouble that God allows in your life.

Forsaking all for the knowledge of Christ

Lord, when I should have been seeking to know you I was chasing after sin and wickedness. I know you created me to love you, but I am bereft of that love. I have lived with my eyes toward the earth, never looking up to you. The corridors of my mind ought to be adorned with portraits of the beauty of your holiness. Instead, I have hung there countless pictures of sinful thoughts and wicked imaginations. Oh, come to me in love and with your precious blood blot these horrible scenes out of my mind. Imprint on my soul your image, blessed Jesus, so that my thoughts will always be fixed on you. Bind my heart to yours so that your will becomes mine. Let me be content to do your will with joy, whatever it may be. May I be fully content with whatever you allow to befall me. Never let me rebel against you even when you chastise me. Permit me to love you passionately and obey you readily. Amen.

Don't become captivated by your own works. Do every good deed with a meek heart and a humble mind. If you think only about your deeds you will lose sight of Christ and your love for him will grow cold. To know him is the greatest pleasure a man can experience. Let your prayer be: 'Transform my will into yours, fill my affections, grant me an insatiable desire to honour you.'

In order to walk in fellowship with the Lord and be ever close to him, you must forsake all sin. The more you are able to live free from the love of this world, the more you will be able to enjoy the Lord your God, and the more completely you will be able to live the heavenly life.

Work to abandon everything that hinders your relationship with Christ. Make it your aim to know and love the Lord Jesus. When you make this your life purpose you will find that he is always on your mind. You will begin to see the providence of God in everything that happens, whether good or bad. This will transform every circumstance into a sweet aroma. Your only desire will then become the praise and honour of Christ.

When deciding what to choose, always choose that which is going to bring the most honour to God. In every situation try to do what Jesus would have done. Do that which is most helpful to your neighbour and least likely to draw attention to yourself.

If you walk faithfully on this path and persistently knock on this spiritual door, without question, God will open it unto you. God will deliver you from your soul's troubles and turmoil. He will free your mind from its vain imaginations.

There are some earthly affections that nothing can kill except the power of a fervent desire to know and love God with all of your heart, soul, mind and strength.

Do not hinder God's working in your life by following your own will. The more you forsake your own will, selfishness, and love of the world, the more you will be joined to God. The more you seek him the more you will come to truly love him.

Rejoicing in tribulation

Oh Jesus my Saviour, engrave your blessed humility on my heart. Help me to be more aware of your infinite glory. For I know that when I truly see you as you are I will see myself clearly as well. When I see myself as I really am I cannot but be humble and readily willing to accept your will in all things. I want to be willing even to be despised and mistreated by others for your sake. Make me able to always say, 'I am nothing, I have nothing, I can do nothing, and I want nothing but you.' Amen.

Whatever happens in life do not allow your heart to move away from God and become bitter. Accept his will and his work with joy in your heart. Don't try to change God's plans to fit your desires. Rather change your plans to conform to his will. If you approach trials with this attitude you will come to know Christ and enjoy him above all else.

Doing God's will needs to be the greatest joy of your heart. Even if doing the will of God involves pain, sickness, grief, darkness, or persecution accept these because you love him. Be careful not to allow these kinds of trials to draw your heart back to sinful living. Don't allow the difficulties of life to tempt you to seek comfort in the empty pleasures of this world. You might even be tempted by trouble to quit serving the Lord. Don't let that happen. If you can, make yourself work, or engage in some profitable spiritual exercise. God will accept this service too.

You should always think of adversity as a sign of God's love for you and a test of your love for him. He only seeks to enrich your life with more of his grace and his gifts. So faithfully persevere and continue to love him more than anything or anyone else.

Give yourself completely to God as a living sacrifice. Return his love for you with love for him. Let his love be your soul's rest and delight. Enjoy the wonderful union with God we have in Jesus Christ. We can be confident that since he has saved us he will fulfil our desire to know and love him. Once you enter into this new life you will find yourself willing to embrace whatever brings honour to his name.

No doubt, when you have done everything you can do for him, you will feel as though you have done nothing at all. You will even be ashamed that you have so imperfectly served a Lord so noble and worthy as Jesus. Therefore, seek to do greater and more perfect works than you have done before. Forget that which is behind you and press forward to that which lies before you.

If you have already come to experience a deep love for Christ and have learned to abide in him, then cling to him with all your might. Do not allow yourself to be tricked into chasing after the vain things of this world. I know that they seem to offer joy, security and satisfaction; but it is all a mirage. Drink from the fountain of Christ and you will satisfy the desires of your soul.

Remember that every good gift is from God. When anything good happens to you be sure and give thanks to him. Give everything you have to him. Give yourself completely to him too. What possible harm can come to you if you have placed yourself under the shelter of his wings? Nothing can touch you there without going through him first.

The closer you get to God the more you will know his everlasting goodness. You will also come to know the true nobleness of your own soul that came from him, and was made to be re-united with him. You will learn that you have been created for the great purpose of communing with God himself.

If you would ascend to the presence of God you must climb up by the wounds of Christ's blessed humanity. There we shall find that we would rather die that commit any sin. When you give your life to Jesus Christ you cast your soul on an infinite sea of goodness. His love is so vast that it will engulf you as an ocean engulfs a single drop of water. When you arrive in heaven you will be forever changed. You will be thinking without thought, knowing without knowledge, loving without love and comprehended by him whom you cannot comprehend.

General thoughts on spiritual growth

Lord, the only thing I want for myself or anyone else is to know and do your perfect will. My heart's constant plea is, 'Lord, what would you have me to do?' Transform my will so that it conforms to your will. Fill and consume my soul with your love and a desire to honour you that never ceases. Amen.

Here are some thoughts about spiritual growth:

1. The desire to please men rules out the ability and desire to please God.

2. If you become too caught up in strenuous activities you will lose your peace of mind.

3. Give all your worries to God and commit everything to his good pleasure. Praise and applaud God in all things small and great. Forget your own will and give yourself cheerfully to the will of God without reservation. Do God's will wholeheartedly in prosperity or adversity, comfort or pain, and life or death.

4. Untie your heart from everything else and bind it to God alone.

5. Meditate continually with love on the life, death, and resurrection of Jesus our Saviour.

6. Do not gossip about other people's failures, just remember your own.

7. Never think too highly of yourself nor despise others.

8. Practice silence and solitude as much as possible. Through God's grace they will keep you from many snares and offences.

9. Pray often to God and seek his help in everything.

10. Let your heart be filled with love for God and others, and do everything in sincere love.

The sum of this is:

1. Always be aware of God's presence.

2. Always rejoice in God's will.

3. Always refer everything to God's glory.

Final thoughts

1. If you love God only a little you will trust God only a
    little, but great love creates a strong confidence.

2. Hope should not make us slack in our duties or
    arrogant about our condition, but it should increase
    our joy in doing God's will, dying to self, and obey-
    ing God.

3. Don't worry about anything. Keep your mind on God
    and desire only to love him and you will find great
    rest for your soul.

4. Always carry these words in your heart: 'My son, let
    me alone possess your heart.'

5. Be faithful to God with a pure mind. Desire and
    meditate on him always as if you and God were the
    only persons that existed in this world. Let your
    whole heart and mind be absorbed in him.

6. Fix your mind on the crucified Saviour and always
    remember his great meekness, love, obedience, purity
    and patience.

7. Meditate on the mighty power and infinite goodness
    of Christ. Remember that he created you, redeemed
    you, saved you, and works within you to produce the
    fruits of holiness, grace and goodness. Think always
    on Jesus and your thoughts will be transformed into
    love.

8.   Let your mind rest from thinking about this world and let it be silent before God. When you do you will find that your heart is a fit place for God to dwell in and to talk with you.

9.   Humility draws you close to God and changes you into a vessel that can receive his grace and his gifts. Oh, but who can say they have this blessed virtue of humility? It is such a difficult task to perfectly put self to death and kill the terrible root of pride.

10.   Commit all things to God's providence. Do not allow anything to enter or abide in your heart but God. Everything in this world is too corrupt to consume your love, capture your mind or trouble your heart. Let the men of this world worry about worldly concerns.

11.   You cannot serve and please two masters. You cannot love two things that are opposed to each other. If you want to know what you love, ask yourself what you think about most of the time. Lose your life and you will find it. Leave this world behind and hold on to Christ. Leave earth and have heaven.

12.   All sin and vice is the fruit of self-will. All virtue and spiritual life springs up and grows as we die to our selves and give ourselves completely to God.